S0-AXO-119

How to Play & Win at Poker

This edition published in 2006

Copyright © Carlton Books Limited 2006

Carlton Books Limited
20 Mortimer Street
London W1T 3JW

All rights reserved. No part of this publication may be reproduced,
stored in a retrieval system, or transmitted in any form or by
any means, electronic, mechanical, photocopying, recording or
otherwise, without the prior permission of the copyright owner
and the publishers.

A CIP catalogue record for this book is available from the
British Library

ISBN 10: 1-84442-163-5
ISBN 13: 978-1-84442-163-3

Editor: Martin Corteel
Project art editor: Luke Griffin
Design: ON FIRE
Production: Lisa French

Printed in Dubai

Dave Woods
Editor-in-Chief of PokerPlayer,
the leading poker magazine
& Matt Broughton

CARLTON
BOOKS

Contents

Poker's been around for a long, long time. Just ask Mel Gibson seen here in the poker flick *Maverick*

Introduction

'Poker is generally reckoned to be America's second most popular after-dark activity. Sex is good, they say, but poker lasts longer.'
AL ALVAREZ (Author, *The Biggest Game in Town*)

With over two hundred million people playing worldwide and almost four million people playing in the UK alone, it's fair to say that poker is the world's biggest game. All across the globe cards are being shuffled, chips are being used as betting collateral and money is exchanging hands. It's taken a lot of people by surprise but it shouldn't have. Poker has all the ingredients of a great game: it's incredibly easy to learn, yet full of incredibly subtle nuances. Add a dollop of luck, which keeps even the best players in the world in check, and you've got a game that was always likely to spread like wildfire. All it needed was a catalyst...

James Spader in the 1993 film *The Music of Chance*

Introduction

Poker isn't a new game and, contrary to popular opinion, it's not even an American game, although Americans made it their own in the twentieth century. So where does it come from?

The history

You can actually trace poker's roots back to a sixteenth-century Persian game called As Nas, which used a 20- or 25-card deck (depending on whether there were four or five players), containing five different suits or subjects – each a court picture card.

The game then travelled through Germany (where it was known as Pochen) and France (Poque) before ending up in America. The most likely route was through the French colonies, via Canada and New Orleans, at the start of the eighteenth century. It then spread from Louisiana along the Mississippi on the steamboats, and

You can thank ancient Persia for poker. The Persian As Nas game was the forerunner of the game we know today

Do you fancy a bit of this?

ultimately across the whole of America.

But if nobody really knows exactly where poker came from, what is indisputable is that the game as we know it sparked into life in Las Vegas as recently as 1970 when Benny Binion, owner of the Horseshoe casino, launched the World Series of Poker (known as the WSOP). This inaugural tournament was played by a mere handful of players, across a number of different poker variants. At the end they all voted for the winner, and the great Johnny Moss was crowned the official world champion. The next year a freezeout structure was employed, which set the rules for tournament play as we know it today. You paid a fixed entry fee, received the same number of chips as everyone else, and played until you went bust or were declared the winner. But, although the World

Benny Binion's Horseshoe Casino, the spiritual home of the World Series of Poker

Series grew steadily year on year, nothing could have prepared Benny Binion for what was to come.

Today

To put it in technical terms, the game has gone ballistic. Poker, and more specifically a game known as the 'Cadillac of Poker', No-Limit Texas Hold'em, has burst out of the casinos and into the home. The Internet is responsible. People suddenly found that instead of having to travel to poker clubs or casinos, which can be hugely intimidating, they could just log on to an online poker site, 24 hours a day, and find people to play against. They didn't even have to play for money. Games using play money and online tutorials made poker even more popular. And the recent growth in television coverage has poured petrol on the flames. Traditionally poker was never a spectator sport. And for good

reason – you couldn't see the cards. Watching poker ranked below sitting still in a darkened room. Then the UK changed everything.

In 1999, 'Late Night Poker' (first broadcast on Channel 4), introduced the glass-topped table that allowed cameras and viewers to see what cards people had been dealt. Suddenly, the game was essential viewing, and poker was on its way to prime-time viewing. The subsequent money that flowed into the game, and the ensuing celebrity endorsement, made the big poker players the superstars – and multi-millionaires – they are today, and propelled the game into the big time.

Cut to today and you can't move for poker paraphernalia. Supermarkets, high street chains and sports shops all stock a wide range of poker-related products, including cards, chips and poker sets. Last Christmas the poker set was the

'Late Night Poker' introduced the glass-topped table to poker in 1999, which enabled hole cards to be seen for the first time

must-have gift, and was in your face wherever you went. You didn't stand a chance.

Access all areas

But that's not the whole story. A big part of poker's popularity lies with the fact that it's totally non-discriminatory. Which other game puts top celebs like Ben Affleck on the same table as the world champ, a housewife and a student, and lets them all play against each other for millions of dollars? Can you imagine teeing off with Tiger Woods or getting in a ring to fight Mike Tyson? Play poker and you can play with the world's best – and possibly beat them. In 2005 the World Series of Poker was won by Joe Hachem, an Australian chiropractor who trousered $7.5 million. And in the two years previous to this, it was won by Greg Moneymaker and Greg Raymer respectively, and both of these

players won their way to the finals via Internet qualifiers. Reading this book might not make you the world champion but it will give you everything you need to play consistently winning poker. And it'll teach you that poker is about having fun. Remember that in the space of just over 100 years, poker has gone from obscurity to one of the most popular and exciting pastimes on the planet. We're about to show you why...

How to read this book

This isn't a novel and we're not trying to win a literary prize. Feel free to jump around and treat it like a reference book. Skip certain chapters and then come back. Flick through the glossary, first learn the etiquette, and then how to bet like a pro. It's up to you. All we would say is that if you're planning on playing for real money, read it all. And then go through it all again.

The symbols

As you read through the book, you'll find the following icons...

TRIVIA!

A little nugget of fascinating information. Don't read it because you have to, read it because you want to be the smartass at the pub.

TIP

A solid bit of advice that will help your game. Commit them all to memory.

Advanced

Feeling brave? Then you might want to read these advanced tips. Feel free to skip these bits until you're a decent player.

WARNING!

Poker comes with its own hidden dangers – make sure you don't fall foul of any of them.

Chris Moneymaker won the World Series of Poker in 2003, turning a modest outlay of $35 into $2.5 million. Next year it could be you

Chapter

The Basics

1

'There are few things that are so unpardonably neglected in our country as poker. The upper class knows very little about it. Now and then you find ambassadors who have sort of a general knowledge of poker, but the ignorance of the people is fearful. Why, I have known clergymen, good men, kind-hearted, liberal, sincere, and all that, who did not know the meaning of a "flush". It is enough to make one ashamed of the species.'

MARK TWAIN

Watch *Lock, Stock and Two Smoking Barrels*, and don't make the same mistake... Learn the basics

In this chapter you'll learn...

That poker is played by everyone – intellectuals, sportsmen, comedians, professionals, students, housewives, husbands, the young and the old. And, in this chapter we're going to teach you the basics, introducing you to key concepts and the all-important hand-rankings. Because you wouldn't want to get on the wrong end of Mark Twain's tongue would you?

What is poker?

That might seem like a stupid question but poker is actually an umbrella term that covers a multitude of subtle and not so subtle variations. Underpinning all of them, though, is the basic poker rule set.

The most popular poker games include Texas Hold'em, Omaha, Five-card Draw, Seven-card Stud, Razz, and Omaha Eight-or-Better. And there are hundreds more that people are playing across the globe at this very minute. The good news is that if you know the basics of poker you'll be able to tackle any of its variants. You might not excel in all of them but you should be able to pick up a game and run with it in minutes.

Basically, all poker games boil down to one single fact: the best five-card hand wins the pot (the amount staked by all the players on the current hand). And, unless you're playing a low game (where perversely the lowest hand wins), all poker games abide by the universal ranking system

below. As you can see from the probabilities of getting dealt one of these hands, the ranking system has been devised mathematically. Study it carefully. It might stop you putting all your chips in the pot chasing a pipe dream.

Hand rankings

These are the different poker hands and the approximate probability of getting dealt them with five random cards.

Hand	Probability
Royal flush	650,000-1
Straight flush	72,200-1
Four-of-a-kind (quads)	4,200-1
Full house	700-1
Flush	510-1
Straight	250-1
Three-of-a-kind (trips)	48-1
Two pair	21-1
One pair	5-2
High card	EVENS

Simple enough for dogs and complex enough for intellectuals. It's time you learnt how to play poker

TIP

Try to memorize the hand-ranking table before you move on. If you're no good at memorizing things, come back to it at the end of each chapter. Make a copy and carry it around with you if need be. Whatever happens, don't get the order wrong and think you're winning when you've already lost. And never take your copy with you to a poker table. It's effectively saying you don't know what you're doing.

Hand rankings

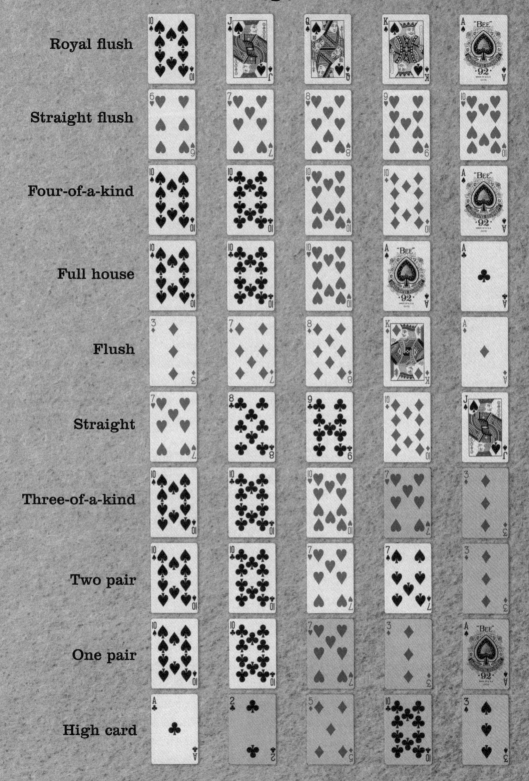

Where two of the same hands come against each other, the higher one wins. So, a pair of Aces will beat a pair of Kings, and an Ace-high flush will win against a King-high flush. If two identical hands are in play (say a pair of Aces against a pair of Aces), the next high card in the hand, known as the kicker, will win. A pair of Aces with a King kicker will beat a pair of Aces with a Queen kicker.

Royal flush

This is the Holy Grail of the poker world and, to give you an idea of its rarity, the authors of this book have clocked up many years of playing and still haven't had one between them. Finding one is still one of their life ambitions. A royal flush is the top five cards – Ten, Jack, Queen, King and Ace – in a single suit. It's the nuts, the best poker hand you can find (unless you're playing Lowball) and can't be beaten. If you do ever get one, you'll probably end up winning $1.50 online with it, not millions in a world championship, but you'll get lots of excited 'WOWS!' from your fellow players which should make you feel very special.

Straight flush

Any other sequence or run of cards of the same suit is known as a straight flush. And unless you're unlucky enough to come up against a royal flush in the same hand you'll win the pot. It's a monster hand. In the unlikely event of two players holding a straight flush in the same hand, the higher card in the hand wins.

Four-of-a-kind

This one doesn't need much explanation – four cards, all of the same rank, such as 10-10-10-10. The higher the rank, the better the hand. Four Aces will beat any other four-of-a-kind, and four Threes will beat four Twos. It's a monster hand so play it accordingly.

Full house

Also known in certain circles as a boat or full boat, a full house is a hand made up of three-of-a-kind and a pair. The three-of-a-kind counts as the higher part of the hand if there are two competing full houses. So a hand made up of Q-Q-Q-8-8 (said to be a full house, Queens full of Eights) would triumph over the hand 8-8-8-Q-Q (a full house, Eights full of Queens). Similarly, a full house A-A-A-10-10 would beat a full house A-A-A-9-9.

Flush

Despite sitting exactly halfway down the rankings ladder, a flush is still a huge hand. It consists of any five cards of the same suit, where the highest card gives the winning hand in the event of two competing flushes. Any flush containing the Ace is known as the 'nut flush' – the best possible flush.

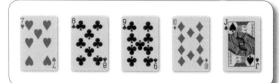

Straight

A sequence of five cards of differing suits (if they were the same suit the hand would qualify as a straight flush or a royal flush). When two straights are competing for the same pot, the highest card in the straight determines the winner. So 4d-5s-6h-7h-8d (an Eight-high straight) beats 2c-3d-4d-5s-6h (a Six-high straight).

Three-of-a-kind

Three cards of the same rank, like J-J-J. Three Jacks beat three Tens, three Aces beat any other three-of-a-kind. It's a good solid hand.

Two pair

A pair of one rank and a pair of another, e.g. A-A and 3-3. If more than one player holds two pair, the rank of the highest pair wins the pot. If both players hold the same highest rank, the one with the best second pair is the winner. A pair of Aces and Threes would beat a pair of Aces and Twos. Two pair seems like a very big hand but depending on the game you're playing and the other cards on the table, it might be extremely dangerous. Look at all the hands that can beat you and play this one with caution.

One pair

A lot of people bet too much on a pair and, while it's true that in games like Texas Hold'em a pair quite often wins, it's important to remember that it's way down in the rankings and only beats a worse pair or a high card. If two people hold pairs the higher pair wins, and if more than one player holds the same pair, the highest unrelated card (or kicker) takes the pot. So a player holding K-K-A-7-8 will beat a player with K-K-J-10-9, with the Ace being the all-important kicker.

High card

Funnily enough you can win a hand with five completely unrelated cards. If no one else makes a pair or better, the high card (Ace being best) wins. Alternatively, you can simply bluff your way out of trouble and try to represent a much stronger hand. Remember that in poker it's not what you've got, but what you make your opponent believe that you've got that's important.

Advanced

Perversely, you can win some games of poker by holding the lowest hand, as in the appropriately named Lowball. And there are some games, such as Omaha Hi/Lo where two hands (the highest and the lowest) can share the pot. It's highly unlikely that you'll play these games as a beginner, but remember that they still follow the basic poker rules using the five-card hands described. It's only the rankings that change.

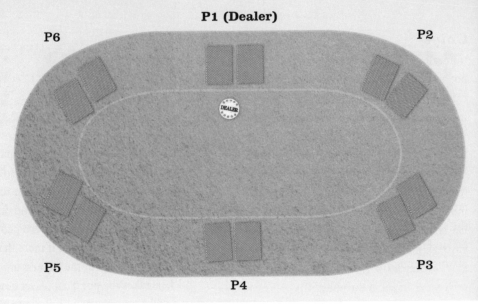

P1 (Dealer)

P6 **P2**

DEALER

P5 **P3**

P4

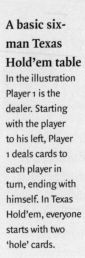

A basic six-man Texas Hold'em table
In the illustration Player 1 is the dealer. Starting with the player to his left, Player 1 deals cards to each player in turn, ending with himself. In Texas Hold'em, everyone starts with two 'hole' cards.

Shuffle up and deal

Most games of poker are played with a standard deck of 52 cards (some variations include a joker) and unlike other games, you always shuffle the deck after each and every hand. You can play on a single table with any number of people from two up to a comfortable maximum of 10 people. In big tournaments, where the field runs into hundreds and thousands, players are split on to individual tables of 10 and these are constantly balanced as people get knocked out.

On each single table, all players take it in turn to act as the dealer. If you're playing online or in a decent casino, a physical or virtual dealer will deal for each of the players on the table, which makes the game quicker and easier. A dealer button is placed in front of the 'current' dealer, and this moves round one place at a time after every hand. This makes it easy to see whose turn it is to deal next, and whose turn it is to place bets. The dealer (or nominal dealer if you're playing online) moves one position clockwise with every hand played and the betting starts with the person directly to the left of the dealer.

Getting started

Betting makes up the core of poker, which is why we've dedicated a whole chapter to it. In fact poker is often described as more of a wagering game (that uses cards as props) than a card game. When you're starting off, play for very low stakes or use play money – most of the online sites let you play for free before graduating to the hard stuff. Why? Because unless you're very lucky, you will start by losing. Even if you win a few games by getting good cards, your first few weeks, or even couple of months, will probably result in a deficit. As soon as you're confident in your own ability, though, you can progress to real money. And that's when poker comes into its own.

///////////////////////////// !

WARNING!
Be sensible. Poker is invariably played for real money, and you should never play for more than you can afford to lose. It's supposed to be a fun game, not something that leaves you destitute. Work out what you can afford to play with and don't be tempted to go above it.

/////////////////////////////

Chips

Ironically, while poker is best played *for* money, it's not best played *with* money. You need a set of poker chips. One of life's great inventions, the chip is your means of keeping score during a game.

Why not just play with money and cut out the middle man? Well, playing with real money is bad for two reasons. Firstly the denominations are all wrong and you can't easily stack or count piles of money. There's nothing that ruins a game of poker like someone going to post a bet and then asking if anyone's got change for a fiver. And if you want to play a game with your friends for the evening and each wants to put in five pounds, how are you going to make that work? You could all go to the bank and come back weighed down with five- and ten-pence

'The guy who invented gambling was bright, but the guy who invented the chip was a genius.'
Julius 'Big Julie' Weintraub
(professional gambler from New York)

Chips are your means of keeping score while you're playing poker

pieces, but would you really want to win a big bag of shrapnel at the end of the night?

There's another very good reason, though, and it's purely psychological. A stack of chips isn't as frightening as a stack of banknotes. You might have all put in £50 to get a stack of brightly coloured chips back in return, but just like foreign currency when you're on holiday, it doesn't feel like you're spending or losing real money. Play at higher stakes and start betting with stacks of notes and you're not going to relax and concentrate on the game. What you'll be thinking is, 'There goes a flat screen TV,' or 'Damn, I could have bought a new pair of shoes with that.' That's no good. And anyway, forgetting the two very important reasons listed above, chips bring poker to life. They provide the sounds (the sound of chips clacking is one you're going to come to love), the colour, the entertainment (when someone tries to riffle and spills them all) and this all conspires to focus your attention on the cards.

Cheap chips are no good either. Play in a casino and you'll play with chunky solid chips that say, 'I'm not messing about here.' They feel good in your hands and you shouldn't play with anything less wherever you are.

Chips don't always equal money

The aim in poker is to win all the chips, and you can do this in one of two ways. You can have the best hand at the showdown (when no more cards are left to be dealt, and the final betting round has finished), or you can make other people think you've got the best hand at any point and make them fold (withdraw from the game) or muck their hands leaving you the last one standing. Either way is good.

Whatever kind of poker game you're playing, you'll be up against other people in what are known as ring (or cash) games or freezeout tournaments. Ring games are where every chip you're betting with has a fixed cash value, and you can win or lose real

Learn some snazzy chip tricks and cultivate a decent table image and you'll have your opponents quaking in their boots

money on every hand. Most pros (who play poker for a living) make most of their money through ring games. You simply take a number of chips to the table and bet on each hand until you're bankrupt or you walk away. Tournaments are different. There's a fixed entry fee, you receive a set number of chips (the same as everyone else), and you play until you've no chips left or you've won every chip in the tournament. These are known as freezeout tournaments and they can be divided further...

Single-table tournament (STT) or sit-and-go

The action takes place on a single table, with anything from 2-10 players. A two-player tournament is known as a heads-up tournament, but no matter how many people you play with, you still follow tournament rules. The prize structure of a single-table, 10-man tournament is usually 50, 30 and 20 per cent of the prize pool for first, second and third places respectively.

In the STT shown opposite, top, 10 players paid $10 each as an entry fee, and received $1,500 worth of chips. Obviously these aren't really worth $1,500, they're just being used to keep the score. Your aim is to knock everyone else out and end up with all

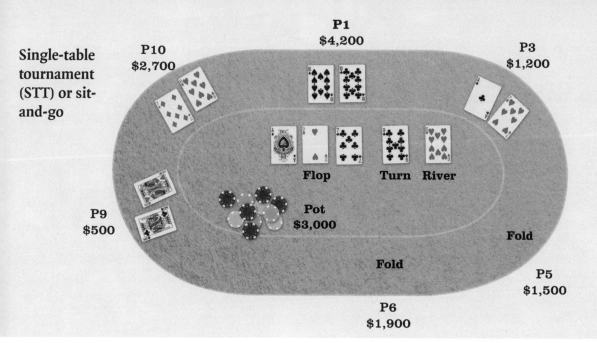

Single-table tournament (STT) or sit-and-go

P10
$2,700

P1
$4,200

P3
$1,200

Flop   Turn River

P9
$500

Pot
$3,000

Fold

Fold

P5
$1,500

P6
$1,900

$15,000 of chips. There are currently six players left – four have busted out (lost all their chips) already, and Player 1 is the chip leader and just about to win a hand.

The STT is a massively popular format for the following reasons. Unlike cash games where you can lose money on each hand, you know exactly how much money you stand to win or lose. Once you've paid your entry fee your liability is over, and you can settle down and enjoy the poker. The STT is also extremely convenient as you can roughly gauge how long you'll be playing. Obviously each game is different, but you can safely say that a 10-man STT

shouldn't take much more than one hour online, or two if you're playing in real life. So you can safely get a quick STT in during your lunch break.

The STT: play until you're out or until you've won all of the chips

Advanced

You can control how long it takes to play a tournament (single- or multi-table) by using different blind structures and starting chip stacks. If you want a quick game you can set fairly high blinds compared to the chips in play and move up through the levels every 10 minutes. If you're looking for a longer game with more play you want to start with low blinds and have longer periods between each raise.

The World Series of Poker is the single biggest tournament in the poker world. Every year thousands of people pack into Harrah's Rio Casino in a bid to be world champion and pocket millions of dollars in prize money

TRIVIA!

The World Series of Poker was originally played at the Horseshoe Casino in downtown Las Vegas, but the size of the event and the fact that it was recently bought out by Harrah's has led to its relocation to the Strip. All 45 of 2006's tournaments took place at the Rio Casino, which saw the biggest festival of poker ever, including the mammoth 13-day Main Event. Ironically, for a card game, it's now acknowledged that you need to be young and fit to survive the gruelling marathon.

Multi-table tournament (MTT)

Most pro players make their living from ring games, but the MTT is where they hit the headlines. These tournaments cover any game of poker where more than one table is in play, so you could have 20 people battling it out across two tables, or 5,000 people in a hall filled with 500 tables. Most MTTs involve the same aim – you've got to accumulate all the chips in play – but the sheer number of players means that you're going to be playing for a lot longer if that's going to happen. Some big tournaments last over a week, and when you consider that you've got to keep your concentration levels at maximum level without making one critical mistake, you can see the challenge.

The biggest tournament is the World Series of Poker which takes place in the air-conditioned halls of Harrah's Rio Casino, Las Vegas, every summer. The 2006 WSOP consisted of 45 different tournaments, including a mixed HORSE event (Hold'em, Omaha, Razz, Seven-card Stud and Eight-or-Better), with a whopping $50,000 entry fee. The main event is still the No-Limit Championship (or The Big One). There's a $10,000 entry fee, but most people qualify online through satellites for as little as $10. The winner is considered the unofficial world champion, and pockets millions of dollars and worldwide fame.

Skill will out

So we've established that poker is a gambling game. In fact some people see poker less as a card game and more of a gambling game with cards as props. Even if you don't play for money you have to have some means of keeping score – like matchsticks. But the beauty of poker is that you're gambling against other people, people just like you – fallible, with wildly varying skill levels and styles of play. You're not playing against the casino, where you're constantly battling against the house advantage, and that's why poker is often referred to as a skill game. Yes, there is an element of luck but good, solid poker will triumph over time.

Checklist

- There are hundreds of different poker variants

- But all of them are betting games where chips are used as collateral

- You win the pot by making the best five-card hand or by bluffing your opponent into folding (giving up)

- The chance of getting a royal flush is about 650,000-1, which means it's still far more likely than winning the lottery

- You can play ring games where chips mean cash, or tournaments (single or multi-table) where you pay a set entry fee and receive the same number of starting chips as everyone else

- Poker is a game of skill played against real people

The multi-table tournaments are where the real money is

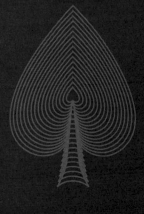

Hold'em

'Hold'em is to Stud and Draw
what chess is to checkers.'
JOHNNY MOSS
(1970, 1971 and 1974 WSOP winner)

In this chapter you'll learn...

How to play by far and away the most popular form of
poker on the planet. Texas Hold'em is the game you see
on TV, read about in the papers and dream about while
you're asleep. Referred to as the 'Cadillac of poker', it's a
mix of nerve, pure adrenaline and psychological warfare,
and it's the most fun you can have with a pack of cards.
Are you ready for the ride of your life?

Michael Imperioli
playing WSOP
champion Stu
Ungar in the
movie *Stuey*

Texas Hold'em

Three words that are guaranteed to light up the eyes and quicken the pulse of any poker player. Texas Hold'em has been growing in popularity since 1970 and has now officially taken over the world.

Thankfully, like all great games, it's extremely easy to learn. And, while some of the stuff we've put in the latter part of this chapter might look a bit complicated, it's really not. Honest.

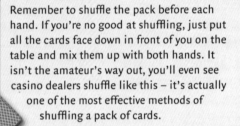

TIP

Remember to shuffle the pack before each hand. If you're no good at shuffling, just put all the cards face down in front of you on the table and mix them up with both hands. It isn't the amateur's way out, you'll even see casino dealers shuffle like this – it's actually one of the most effective methods of shuffling a pack of cards.

As with all poker games, you start by selecting a dealer, usually by drawing for a high card. The deal moves one place clockwise after each hand, and the dealer button is placed in front of the nominated player to keep track of who is dealing. This is known as being 'on the button'.

Before the cards are dealt, the two players to the left of the dealer have to make (or post) forced bets known as the small and big blinds. These bets 'force' the action, and mean that there's always something to play for on the table. Without them, there'd be nothing to stop everyone waiting until they're dealt a premium starting hand, which would make the game exceptionally dull to play. The big blind

Getting started

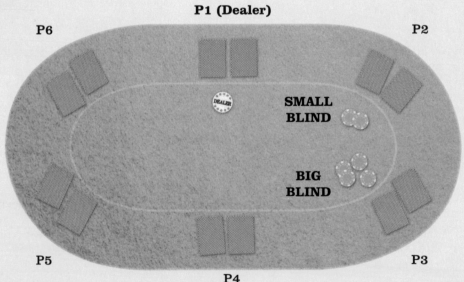

Here you can see the position of the dealer and the two forced bets, known as the blinds, to the left of him. Everyone has two cards, which means it's time for the first round of betting.

P1 (Dealer)

P6

P2

DEALER

SMALL BLIND

BIG BLIND

P5

P3

P4

represents the amount of the first bet that must be matched – or raised – by players wanting to stay in the hand.

Once the blinds have been posted, the dealer gives a card face down to all the players, in turn, at the table, starting with the player to his left, until every player has two cards face down in front of them. These two cards are known as your hole cards, and they're the only cards that are unique to you. Look after them.

When every player has two hole cards, it's time for the first round of betting. The betting starts with the player to the left of the big blind, who must either call the bet (match the amount posted by the big blind), raise or fold his hand. This continues around the table until all the players have either matched the largest bet, or folded. If there's no raise, the big blind has the option of raising or checking (making no bet).

The flop

Next comes the most critical phase in any hand of Texas Hold'em, the flop. After 'burning' a single card face down, the dealer deals three cards face up in the middle of the table. Collectively they are known as the flop, and they can be used by all of the players at the table to help make their five-card poker hand. If you're still in the game, you're now in possession of five out of the seven cards you get in total. That's why most hands are either made or broken at the flop.

After the flop comes another round of betting, this time starting with the person sitting directly to the left of the dealer who can check (make no bet and pass the action round), bet or fold. As first to act you don't have to put a bet at this stage, there's no point in folding – you might as well check and try to see the turn card for free.

Once the betting round is over, the dealer burns another card face down and then deals the fourth

TIP

It might seem like an utterly trivial point, but it's important to develop a good technique for looking at your hole cards. If you watch pros playing on TV, you'll see that they 'squeeze' the corners of their cards up, using the corner indices to clock the cards. Do this and it makes it impossible for any other player to see what you've got, and marks you down as someone who's played the game before. Pick them up and hold them in front of your eyes and you'll find everyone else at the table eyeing you up and licking their lips. And no one wants that.

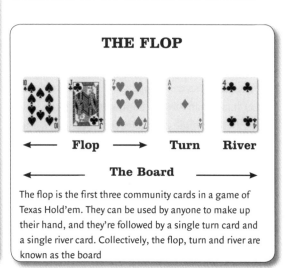

THE FLOP

← **Flop** → **Turn** **River**

← **The Board** →

The flop is the first three community cards in a game of Texas Hold'em. They can be used by anyone to make up their hand, and they're followed by a single turn card and a single river card. Collectively, the flop, turn and river are known as the board community card (the turn) face up. There's another round of betting, and another burn card, before the fifth and final community card (the river).

At this point, everyone left in the game has got two hole cards and five community cards to make up their best five-card hand. You can use any of these seven cards to make up your final hand, with either both or one of your hole cards, or none if there's a better hand showing on the board (called playing the board). Now that all the cards are in play, the final round of betting takes place, and if more than one player is left in following this, the cards are revealed – the showdown – and the winner (according to the hand rankings on page 14) scoops the pot. The nature of the game means that a lot of hands don't get this far.

TRIVIA!
In a live game of Texas Hold'em, the dealer always 'burns' (places a card face down) a single card before the flop, turn and river. This is done to avoid cheats using a marked deck to their advantage. With a marked deck, the cheat would know the identity of the next card before each round of betting.

Split pots

A split (or shared) pot happens when the winning hand is held by two or more players at the showdown. This can happen if the board shows a better hand than anyone contesting it. In the first of our two examples you have a pair of Kings and your opponent a pair of Eights, while the board is 10-10-10-10-A, giving both of you four-of-a-kind with an Ace kicker. None of your cards can improve this, and the pot is split.

Another common split pot occurs when two or more players hold the same card with a weak kicker. In the second example, you hold A-7 and

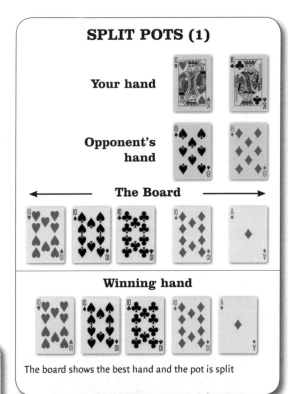

SPLIT POTS (1)

Your hand

Opponent's hand

The Board

Winning hand

The board shows the best hand and the pot is split

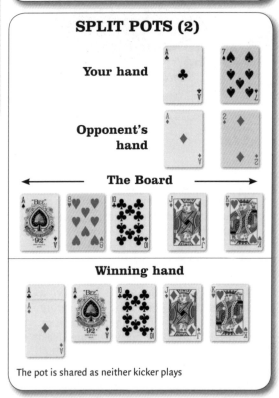

SPLIT POTS (2)

Your hand

Opponent's hand

The Board

Winning hand

The pot is shared as neither kicker plays

your opponent A-2. The board shows A-8-10-J-K. You both have a pair of Aces, but your kicker (the 7) isn't higher than any of the cards on the board. This means that the highest possible hand – and the one that applies to both you and your opponent – is A-A-10-J-K.

Texas Hold'em strategy

And that's all there is to Texas Hold'em. But, while it's extremely easy to learn how to play, it's a bit harder to learn how to play well. What follows is basic strategy. Practise it, and you'll be able to hold your own in most low-level games, but remember there's no substitute for experience. You can read all the textbooks in the world, but unless you play, play and play some more you'll only ever be a theoretical champion.

Premium starting hands

You get seven cards in total to make up your final hand in Texas Hold'em, but only two of them are unique to you – the hole cards you receive at the start. That's why the starting hands are critical to your success. Until you get the hang of the game, we'd advise you to stick to playing only the following premium hands. Remember, though, that none of them guarantees winning the pot.

A-A

Unquestionably the strongest starting hand in Texas Hold'em; look down at a pair of Aces and you'll have to stop your heart doing cartwheels. Also known as 'pocket rockets', they're one of the sweetest sights in poker. Don't get carried away though. At the end of the day you've still only got a pair, albeit the highest possible pair. Beware of danger flops that point to straights or flushes.

K-K

The cowboys are the second strongest pair in Texas Hold'em, and also the second strongest hand you can be dealt. Play them accordingly, but be wary of an Ace hitting the flop (something that will happen approximately one in five times). If you raise your bet before the flop with Kings, there's a big chance that the player that calls or raises the bet is holding an Ace. Be prepared to throw them away if you think you're beat.

Q-Q

The third strongest pair in the game, but with Kings and Aces as overcards you have to be prepared to drop them if the flop shows either of them. Never get so attached to a hand that you can't walk away from it. It's the quickest route to going bust.

J-J

The last of the big pairs and the most problematic to play. Jacks are in big trouble against Aces, Kings and Queens on the flop. In fact if two players stay in and hold all three overcards between them, you're in very bad shape. Watch your opponent's bets and beware the flop. Remember, never get attached to a losing hand.

10-10, 9-9, 8-8

All of these pairs can be extremely hard to play, but they can also be very powerful. If there's been no action before your betting turn, you should raise and pay extra close attention to the rest of the table's betting patterns. Big reraises made before your turn should make you worried, and could be enough to make you fold before seeing the flop. When the flop is revealed, what you really want to see is the magic card that gives you three-of-a-kind, but even if this doesn't happen you could still have the winning hand.

A-K

Also known as big slick, A-K can be a monstrously big hand, especially when the two cards are of the same suit, but you still need to improve. If you don't hit an Ace or a King, or make a straight or a flush, you've only got an Ace high in your hand and that's not going to scare anyone. Bet or raise before the flop and try to thin the field down to one person if possible. If in doubt, try and remember the other nickname the poker community has given to the hand – Anna Kournikova. A-K might look great but it doesn't always play well.

A-Q, A-J, A-10

All three are strong starting hands depending on the number of players at the table (the more players, the weaker the hands become), and the amount of action before your turn to bet. Bear in mind that a big bet, raise or reraise could signify A-A, K-K, Q-Q or A-K, all four of which would dominate you horribly if you got involved.

K-Q, K-J, Q-J, Q-10

Go ahead and play, depending on the number of people at the table and your position relative to the button. Position is paramount in Hold'em, and hands become much stronger the closer you are to the dealer's button.

Remember that the strength of your hand goes up as the number of players on the table goes down. Qh-10h probably isn't worth playing on a full 10-man table in early position but if you're playing heads-up (a two-player tournament) or everyone's folded round to you on the small blind it's a veritable monster.

Playing big pairs

As you only get two hole cards, it follows that the best starting hands you can get are big pairs. But, while they're great starting hands, they can also get you into trouble if you don't play them properly. Get dealt a pair of Aces and your first instinct might be to tempt everyone into the pot to maximize your winnings. This is a huge mistake. Aces might be a massive favourite against any other single hand, but add three or four random hands to the mix and suddenly you're the underdog with a real chance of losing all of your chips.

In the first example (top right), you're first to bet and flat-call the big blind with your Aces. Player 4 bets with 10s-Js, Player 5 calls with Kh-9h and the two blinds limp in and check respectively with 8s-6s and 7d-3h.

Playing big pairs

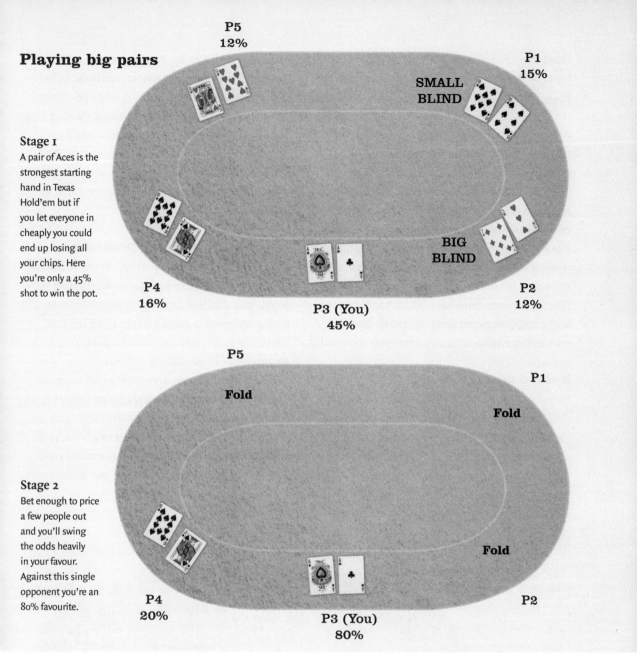

P5
12%

P1
15%

SMALL BLIND

BIG BLIND

P4
16%

P2
12%

P3 (You)
45%

Stage 1
A pair of Aces is the strongest starting hand in Texas Hold'em but if you let everyone in cheaply you could end up losing all your chips. Here you're only a 45% shot to win the pot.

P5

P1

Fold

Fold

Fold

Stage 2
Bet enough to price a few people out and you'll swing the odds heavily in your favour. Against this single opponent you're an 80% favourite.

P4
20%

P2

P3 (You)
80%

Approximate chance of winning pre-flop

Player 1:	8s-6s	15 per cent
Player 2:	7d-3h	12 per cent
You:	As-Ac	45 per cent
Player 4:	10s-Js	16 per cent
Player 5:	Kh-9h	12 per cent

As you can see, the Aces are still the single biggest favourite, but you're now the underdog against the rest of the hands combined. Since it doesn't matter who takes your money if you lose, it means you're no longer the favourite to win the hand. And from the strongest starting position, that's not a good move.

Now look what happens if you replay that hand but put in a decent raise of three times the big blind. Player 4 still calls with his 10-J suited, but the rest of the players fold leaving you to contest the pot against one other player.

Approximate chance of winning pre-flop

You:	As-Ac	80 per cent
Player 4:	10s-Js	20 per cent

As you can see you're now an 80 per cent favourite to take the pot. You might still get outdrawn and lose but you've put yourself in a winning position, and that's what Texas Hold'em is all about. Obviously the same goes for all big pairs, but thinning down the field is even more important. When you're holding Kings and Queens you don't want to go against multiple opponents who might be holding overcards.

Suited connectors

Suited connectors are two cards of the same suit that can link to form straights. The shorter the gap, the better the connection. A hand like 8h-9h is going to give you more chance of making a straight than 4h-8h.

Suited connectors are extremely popular with a lot of Hold'em players as they let you make huge hands with harmless-looking flops like 6d-7h-10s, as well as offering flush possibilities. If this happens you can slow down the play and try to take your opponent for everything he's got. You need to be extremely careful playing hands like this though, and to start we'd recommend sticking to the premium hands we mentioned earlier.

Position, position, position

But, while playing with premium starting hands is a safe and solid way to Texas Hold'em, the problem is that you're going to be very easy to read. Ideally you want to mix your play up and, when you're comfortable with the game, you should think about widening the net.

The important thing to remember is that in Texas Hold'em position is paramount. The closer you are to the button, the more hands you can play, and the wilder you can be. It might be hard to grasp when you first start, but if you're on the button (the dealer), you're the last to act in all

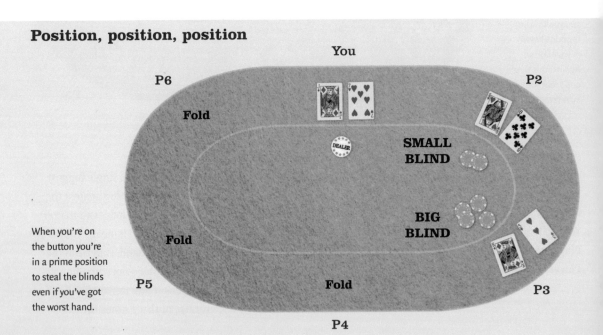

Position, position, position

You

P6

Fold

P2

DEALER

SMALL
BLIND

BIG
BLIND

When you're on the button you're in a prime position to steal the blinds even if you've got the worst hand.

Fold

P5

Fold

P3

P4

betting rounds from the flop onwards. (In the first round of betting the small and big blinds are the last to bet, but they're first to bet in all subsequent rounds.) This means that you get to see what the other players are doing and their relative strengths. Play to your position and you'll become a much better Hold'em player.

Your hand: Jd-7h
Small blind: Qh-8c
Big blind: Kd-3h

Here you've got a pretty poor hand, but everyone at the table has folded round to you on the button. This means that you've only got two players – the small and big blinds – to beat, and the chances of them holding a premium hand are slim. Despite the fact that both of them have got you beaten, a raise 'on the button' may well take the pot uncontested. And remember, if you get called you've still got a chance of connecting on the flop and winning the hand.

If you want to play aggressively you can take this a step further and raise with anything on the button in the hope of the two blinds folding. Be careful how often you try this though, as the blinds will eventually get sick of you stealing and make a stand.

To play or not to play

If you make a strong hand on the flop in Texas Hold'em your decision is easy. But what if you flop a marginal or drawing hand. How much should you commit to the pot?

Bottom pair

On the following flop you've connected, but you've only made bottom pair. That means there are two overcards on the board and, if your opponent holds either, he's a huge favourite. As it happens he's made top pair and is a big favourite.

BOTTOM PAIR

Your hand — 25%

Opponent's hand — 75%

The Flop

Here you've hit bottom pair, but your opponent is a massive favourite with a pair of Jacks

Approximate percentage chance of a winning hand
Your hand: As-7c   25 per cent
Player 2:   Kh-Jh   75 per cent
Flop: 7s-Js-8d

One of the fundamentals of poker is not to get caught up in a hand where you're probably losing. Beware the overcards, and watch out for betting in front of you. If you're the first to act you could put out an exploratory bet, but only one that you're prepared to lose if you get raised.

Drawing hands

What if you make a hand that needs to improve, like a straight or a flush draw? Fortunately, it's extremely easy to work out your chances of making a hand using simple maths. All you need to do is calculate the number of cards left in the pack that you need to make your hand. These are known as your outs. If you're looking at the flop, with the turn and river to come, you need to multiply the number of outs by four. If you're just waiting for the river, you multiply your outs by two and add two. While the figures you get

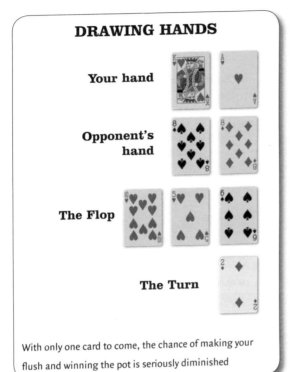

DRAWING HANDS

Your hand

Opponent's hand

The Flop

The Turn

With only one card to come, the chance of making your flush and winning the pot is seriously diminished

aren't mathematically exact, you can calculate up to 14 outs without being any more than 5 per cent out – and above 14 outs with the turn and river to come, you're always a favourite to make the hand. Either way it's close enough to satisfy all but the most anal poker player.

Your hand: Kh-Ah
Flop: 10h-5h-6s

Here you've flopped a potential monster winning hand. You've got four out of the five cards needed to make your nut flush (you have the Ace, so no other flush can beat you). It looks like a no-brainer, but Player 1 in front of you has pushed in all of his chips, which means that you'll have to do the same to stay in the pot. Is it still a no-brainer?

There are 13 hearts in the deck. You've got two and there are another two on the flop, leaving nine in the pack (you can't assume that any other player

has a heart). So, your chance of hitting one of the remaining hearts is 9x4=36 per cent. There's just over a 1 in 3 chance that you're going to complete the flush, which suddenly makes the act of pushing in all your chips that much harder. Do you gamble or not? You decide.

In this instance though, you might also think that another Ace or a King would win it for you as well, giving you a further six outs, making 15 in total (the three remaining Aces and the three remaining Kings). This pushes your odds up to 15x4=60 per cent, which swings things back in your favour.

But when you move on to the river, the odds are stacked against you. Take the very same hand, but now you've been pushed all-in following the turn, and the board looks like this.

Board: 10h-5h-6s-2d

The odds to hit the flush are now 9x2+2=20 per cent, and the odds to hit either a flush or an Ace or King are 15x2+2=32 per cent. Suddenly folding looks like the best course of action.

Now you might be thinking that you didn't get into poker to learn maths, and you'd be right. Poker is supposed to be fun and we're not advising that you play your game with a calculator in hand. But if you learn the basic probabilities you'll know when to gamble and when to fold, and you'll wind up winning more games. And that's where the fun starts.

Pot odds

Question: When should you draw to a hand that you're not a favourite to make? Answer: When the pot, or what you stand to win, is offering you favourable odds (known as pot odds). In the following hand you're drawing to a flush which means that you have nine cards left in the deck that can help you.

POT ODDS

Your hand

The Flop and Turn

Pot: $5,000

Bet to call: $500   Pot odds 10-1

Odds to hit flush approx: 20%   4-1

Verdict: Call

In this situation you should draw at the flush even though you're only a 20% shot. You're getting the right odds

Your hand: Ac-Qc
Flop and Turn: 6c-9c-2h-4d
Percentage chance of making the flush:
9x2+2=20 per cent

You're the last to act and Player 1 has just made a bet of $500, a bet you must match to stay in the hand. As you have a 20 per cent chance of making the nut flush, for every five hands that are dealt you'll make it once and fail to make it four times. That means you should call when the pot is at least four times the size of the bet you're making. In this instance there is already $5,000 in the pot – ten times the size of the bet you'd have to make to stay in, which means you should make the call. This is known as pot odds, and a basic understanding of this will make you a better player. In effect you're playing a percentage game, using basic maths to work out how to end on the winning side more often than not.

Aggression

Aggression pays in Texas Hold'em, and some of the most successful players in the world employ it with lethal force – especially against passive opponents. In the following example you've been dealt 7-3 off-suit yet you decide to raise pre-flop, forcing all the other players to fold except Player 2 who calls with A-K.

Your hand: 7s-3h
Player 2: Ah-Kh
Flop: 2s-10d-8c

The flop comes down with blanks yet you make another bet, knowing that Player 2 is a tight player who only bets when he has got the best hand. As expected, he folds his superior hand. Remember, you don't have to have the best hand in Texas Hold'em, you just have to convince your opponent that you have. And being aggressive can be devastating in big tournaments where players are reluctant to lose their chips. Say you've scraped together $10,000 to enter the World Series and, on the first day, you're put in the position of Player 2 and asked to risk all of your chips on a hand which you haven't connected with. Would you push them in? Thought not.

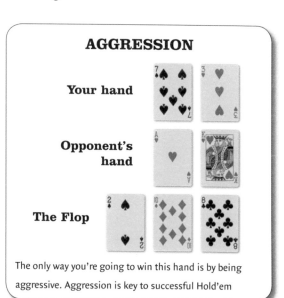

AGGRESSION

Your hand

Opponent's hand

The Flop

The only way you're going to win this hand is by being aggressive. Aggression is key to successful Hold'em

TIP

Aggressive play works in Texas Hold'em, and if you constantly limp into pots you're likely to be bet off a large proportion of them by more aggressive players. Former world champion, Chris Ferguson, has an eloquent way of putting it, 'Pump 'em or dump 'em.' His philosophy is that if a hand's worth calling with, it's worth raising with. Try it out for yourself and you'll be amazed at how many pots you can take down uncontested, even with awful cards.

Bluffing in Hold'em

With the five community cards, Texas Hold'em is ripe for bluffing. In the following example you're holding top pair and are way ahead in the hand when an Ace drops on the turn.

Your hand:	Kc-10c
Player 2:	10s-7h
Flop:	3s-Kd-4h
Turn:	As

BLUFFING

Your hand

Opponent's hand

The Flop

The Turn

Even though you're winning the hand, the Ace is a danger card your opponent can represent

Your opponent hasn't got an Ace but he's pretty sure you haven't either, and fires off a large bet. This is called 'representing', and it's a common and extremely effective tactic in Texas Hold'em. How can you know if your opponent has an Ace or not? There's no way of being 100 per cent sure but, by watching betting patterns and looking out for tells you can make an educated guess. If you can afford it you could always call his bluff and reraise him. If he hasn't got the Ace he'll most likely fold so fast you won't even see his cards until they're in the muck.

Want some more?

Hold'em plays by fairly strict maths and you can improve your game by knowing the basics. Check out the three tips below, and mess around with an odds calculator (there's one at www.pokerplayermagazine.co.uk) to get more fascinating stats. For instance, did you know that a pair of Aces is an 80 per cent favourite over any other pair, or that any pair going against two other higher cards has roughly a 50-50 chance of winning? And how about this: a pair of Twos is a favourite against A-K, but a slight underdog against 10-J. Strange but true...

TIP

Try and burn these three useful facts into your subconscious and you'll be ahead of most of your opponents round the table...

• If you've got a pair there's approximately an 8-1 chance of making three-of-a-kind on the flop.

• Get dealt A-K and you'll connect with another Ace or King on the flop about one in three times.

• Two suited cards will make a flush approximately 7 per cent of the time – and you'll flop a flush less than 1 per cent of the time. Don't get blinded by two cards of the same suit.

Omaha

It is entirely feasible to play Texas Hold'em and nothing but Texas Hold'em for the rest of your days, and never get bored. But do this and you're missing out on the game that provides action by the bucketload.

Omaha is the second most popular poker game in the world and, at first glance, looks very similar to Texas Hold'em. In fact, in its basic structure and approach it is, but scrape the surface and it's an entirely different beast. The most basic difference is that instead of two hole cards, each player is dealt four hole cards (which can only be played by that person).

The same but different

After this, the game follows the same structure: a round of betting is followed by the flop, another round of betting before the turn, another before the river, and then the final round of betting. And on this basis many a Texas Hold'em player has blundered into Omaha and been badly burned. Because, despite the similarities, subtle nuances in the rules make it a wholly different prospect.

Two from four

And all of the differences come from the four hole

OMAHA HOLD'EM
Four hole cards

Get dealt four hole cards and you know you're playing Omaha

cards and the crucial fact that in Omaha you have to use two and only two of these cards to make up your final hand. What this means is that...

· **Your cards are physically harder to handle**
Now you might think that sounds like a joke, but if you're used to manipulating and peeking at two cards, try it with four. It's not that easy, especially when you might have to keep looking back at them as the game develops, without giving away crucial information to your opponents. Beginners even make the folly of picking up their cards and putting them in numerical order, which is a bit like flashing a sign above your head screaming 'Easy Money'.

· **Omaha pots are generally won with much higher hands than in Texas Hold'em**
There are physically more cards in play and the different combinations you and your opponents hold mean that monsters come along much more frequently. Keep holding out to the showdown with a pair and you're going to empty your pockets quicker than a trip to a roulette table.

· **But the most important difference comes from the simple fact that you have to play two, and no more than two, of your hole cards**
Remember that in Texas Hold'em you can play all or none of your hole cards, depending on what's on the table. Not in Omaha, and this one simple quirk completely alters the game. Why?

Look at your hole cards and see four of a kind.

Good? Incorrect. As you can only use two of the four cards you've got in your hand, the best you're going to have at the showdown is a pair. (And as you'll know, if you've read these points in order, a pair isn't that good in Omaha.) You can't make a flush or a straight as you've got to use two of the cards from your four (and no

straight or flush contains a pair), and you can't make three of a kind as you've got the other two in your hand. So four Twos is the worst starting hand you can get dealt in Omaha. And it's for this reason that there's no set list of starting hands that are considered the strongest. In fact, given the combinations that come from the four cards (using two and only two, each player has up to six starting combinations), few Omaha starting hands have a big advantage over any other.

In Texas Hold'em it's easy to see which starting hand is the clear favourite. In Omaha it's a lot closer, as you can see from the following hands.

Player 1:	As-Ad-9c-10c	30 per cent
Player 2:	5c-Jh-3h-4h	18 per cent
Player 3:	5s-6s-Qh-Kh	31 per cent
Player 4:	7c-8c-10s-10d	20 per cent

At first glance you'd be forgiven for thinking that Player 1 would hold a big advantage, with a pair of Aces and suited connectors. In actual fact, Player 3, with two suited connectors (two flush possibilities with the two spades and the two hearts) is a marginal favourite. None of the four hands is streets ahead though, and that's why Omaha provides much more action than a game of Hold'em where folding pre-flop is much more common. Bluffing is less prevalent as well. That''s not to say that bluffing doesn't happen – it does – but you need to be a very aggressive, confident and adept player to make it work.

Usually, the nut, or very close to the nut, hand will win and, because of the number of cards and combinations in play, this hand is usually much higher than a winning Hold'em hand. Now for the bad news. If you hate maths, odds and probabilities, steer clear. In the absence of bluffing, and because Omaha is usually played in limit or pot-limit form where the best hand changes all the time, Omaha does rely heavily on maths. Don't like it? Stick to Texas Hold'em.

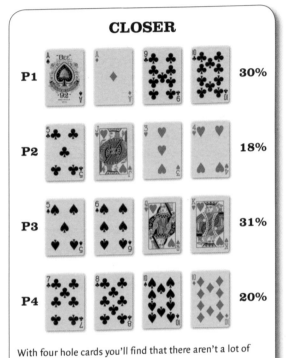

CLOSER

P1 ... 30%

P2 ... 18%

P3 ... 31%

P4 ... 20%

With four hole cards you'll find that there aren't a lot of starting hands that are a big favourite

TIP

You're looking at a board with four hearts on it. You've got two hearts in your hand but are worried that others are going to make higher flushes. Any bet in Texas Hold'em would make your hand a must-fold, but in Omaha your opponent has to have two hearts in his hand to make the flush. He can't use four from the board, only three, and two from his hand. The fact that you've got at least two, and the four on the board, make it far less likely that this is the case.

Premium starting hands

What makes up a premium starting hand in Omaha? It's important that all your cards work well together. So, a hand of 10-J-Q-K (with two different suits) is excellent. What you don't want is a hand with one completely unconnected card, like A-K-J-4. The Four in this hand is known as a dangler, and like most other danglers, it's something you don't want to see in your hand. Effectively you've lost a quarter of your hand from the start, which puts you at a big disadvantage.

If you're still not sure what makes up a good Omaha hand, look for the following...

· high cards
· connecting cards (for straights)
· cards that could draw to the nut flush
· cards that could draw to quads or full houses

High or Hi/Lo

Still with us? Good, because things are about to get even more complicated. Omaha is played in two different formats, Omaha High and Omaha Hi/Lo (also known as Eight-or-Better). Omaha High is easy to understand because it follows the same basic rules as Texas Hold'em, where the highest hand wins the pot. But in Omaha Hi/Lo the pot is split between the highest and the lowest hands, as long as a low hand qualifies.

For a low hand to qualify it must contain five cards with nothing higher than an Eight. Aces count high or low, and flushes and straights are ignored for the low hand, so the lowest hand is therefore A-2-3-4-5. The same Omaha rules apply, so you have to use two cards from your hand and, for a low to exist, there must be three cards Eight or lower on the table. If there's no qualifying low hand, the high hand takes the lot. It's definitely a game to dump on your unsuspecting mates during a home game. They won't know what hit 'em.

Checklist

- Texas Hold'em is the most popular game of poker; it's extremely easy to learn the basics but incredibly hard to master

- Position and selection of starting hands are paramount

- You shouldn't slow-play big pairs

- Or draw to improbable hands

- Aggression normally pays off

- A basic knowledge of probabilities is essential

- If you've been dealt four cards you're playing Omaha

- Where hands are stronger and maths plays a much bigger part

- If you're playing Omaha Hi/Lo you're an extremely brave person

Stud

'Try to decide how good your hand is at a given moment. Nothing else matters. Nothing!'
DOYLE BRUNSON (Professional Poker Player)

In this chapter you'll learn...

That Stud is probably the most complicated poker variant there is. It's played with a mixture of concealed and exposed cards, which means that there's a massive amount of information that the best players will use to their advantage. If you want to succeed you'll have to be disciplined and prepared to concentrate, and there are a number of deep strategies you'll need to master and popular variations to learn before you can call yourself a player. And more than with any other game you'll have to be prepared to drop hands once you think they're losing. And that's not easy...

Steve McQueen playing Stud in the classic film *The Cincinnati Kid*

Stud Poker

Before Texas Hold'em became so powerful in the world of poker, Seven-card Stud was the game to play. A very different game from Hold'em, it requires patience, a great deal of attention and an analytical mind.

If that sounds like you, Stud could be the poker game you've been craving. A lot of Stud players swear by the game, sneering at the simplistic Hold'em. When you're playing Stud, besides checking your own hand, you need to be completely aware of all the cards on the table, including each and every card your opponent has on show. Though some cards are concealed, the majority are exposed, giving a wealth of information that you need to keep track of. It's a far more complicated game of poker and should only be played when you are rested, focused and able to give it 100 per cent.

Stud games are defined by some simple details. There are no community cards, but some of the players' cards are exposed to all. Five-card variants are played, but by far the most popular is Seven-card Stud

How to play

Seven-card Stud is generally a fixed-limit game played with between two and eight players, and to start everyone has to post an ante (generally one-quarter of the lower limit) which goes into the initial pot. After posting their antes, each player

SEVEN-CARD STUD

┌──── Round 1 ────┐			2	3	4	5
Pocket/Hole		Door	4th Street	5th Street	6th Street	River

Stud is often described as a 'series of streets' because of the number of betting rounds.

receives three cards, two concealed and one face-up. This is called third street. The player now showing the lowest card must make a forced bet of either half the lower limit (what's known as the bring-in bet) or the full lower-limit amount. All the other players in sequence – beginning with the player to the left of the player who made the first bet – have to fold, call or raise.

If the starting player only bets the bring-in, the other players can chose to call this amount or complete the bet to the lower limit. In this round of betting, units are set at the lower limit, so, in a $1/2 game, all bets and raises would be in increments of $1. As with many limit games, you're only allowed a maximum of three raises before the pot is considered capped, and that

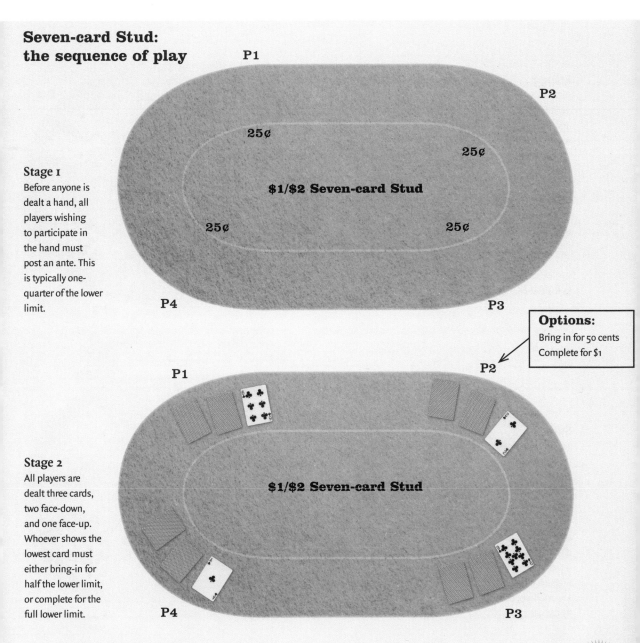

Seven-card Stud: the sequence of play

P1

P2

25¢

25¢

$1/$2 Seven-card Stud

25¢

25¢

P4

P3

Stage 1
Before anyone is dealt a hand, all players wishing to participate in the hand must post an ante. This is typically one-quarter of the lower limit.

Options:
Bring in for 50 cents
Complete for $1

P1

P2

$1/$2 Seven-card Stud

P4

P3

Stage 2
All players are dealt three cards, two face-down, and one face-up. Whoever shows the lowest card must either bring-in for half the lower limit, or complete for the full lower limit.

betting round is closed. (See the chapter on Betting for the full low-down on betting in limit games and capping.)

In the fourth street all players receive a fourth card face-up, and betting in this round begins with the player who shows the highest hand. He can check or bet, with the minimum bet dictated by the lower limit. The exception to this rule is if a pair is exposed. In this case the active player can chose to bet either the lower or higher limit. If the player opts to make a bet at the higher limit, all other bets and raises must be at the same level.

Fifth street is now dealt to all players, again, face-up. From this betting round on, all bets must be made in increments of the higher limit. Sixth street is identical, and the seventh card dealt to the players – the river – is a final concealed card. Following one final round of betting, any

Stage 3
All players are now dealt fourth street, and a betting round starts with the highest cards shown. Because a pair is exposed the player can choose to lead the betting with the lower or higher limit. If there was no exposed pair, the betting would stick to the lower limit.

Options:
• Check $1
• Bet $1

$1/$2 Seven-card Stud

Stage 4
All players are now dealt fifth street, and the betting round is initiated again by the highest showing hand. From this round onwards, all betting is in increments of the higher limit. Sixth street follows, bound by the same rules.

Options:
• Check
• Bet $1

$1/$2 Seven-card Stud

remaining players showdown (i.e. reveal their cards), and the player with the highest five-card poker hand from his seven cards wins the pot. As you can see from the simple example below, there are lots of cards in play at any one time. This means that on a full table it can be hard to keep track of all the exposed cards, and how your opponents' hands are developing compared to yours. In a live game this is even more strenuous

TIP

If two players show the same low card at 'third street', the suit ranks can be used to break the tie. The suit strengths are, from strongest to weakest, Spades-Hearts-Diamonds-Clubs.

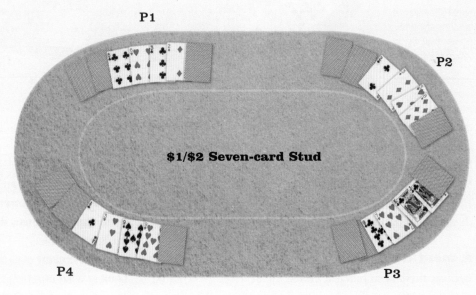

Stage 5
After sixth street and its subsequent betting round, the final card – the river – is dealt to each player face-down. One final round of betting takes place as before.

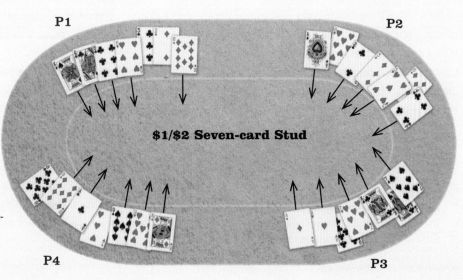

Stage 6
Once all the betting rounds have concluded, all active players show their complete hands, selecting their best five-card hands from the seven cards to which they have access.

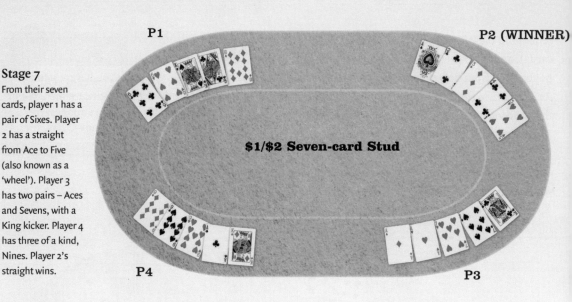

Stage 7

From their seven cards, player 1 has a pair of Sixes. Player 2 has a straight from Ace to Five (also known as a 'wheel'). Player 3 has two pairs – Aces and Sevens, with a King kicker. Player 4 has three of a kind, Nines. Player 2's straight wins.

P1

P2 (WINNER)

$1/$2 Seven-card Stud

P4

P3

because it seems like every inch of the table is covered in cards, but it's crucial that you use all the information available. If a player is showing a pair, but the other two cards of that rank are exposed, you know that he can't possibly improve up to three-of-a-kind.

A mental checklist

Because there is so much action at the Seven-card Stud table, you need to develop your own internal systems and processes to keep track of the information. As players fold out of the round, their cards will be taken by the dealer. If you don't memorize what has already been exposed, you'll be at a disadvantage to more diligent players. If you ever feel that you have totally lost track of a hand's progress, let it go.

TIP

The most critical decision in Seven-card Stud is deciding whether you should proceed after the first three cards are dealt. If these three cards don't give you a lot of options then they're not worth playing.

Here's a checklist of the things you should be looking out for.

- **Cards:** After the initial deal, and before anyone has the opportunity to fold, try to register as many door (face-up) cards as possible.
- **Suits:** Count how many of each suit are out.
- **Rank:** Look at what numbers are out.
- **Bring-in:** Make a mental note if the player bringing-in calls any raises.
- **Raisers:** Note who – if anyone – is the first player to make a raise.

All of these points should take priority over checking your own hand. The good news is that your hand won't go anywhere until you decide what to do. Some of the information available to you elsewhere could soon be gone, and the more you've taken in, the more powerful your position. A player being dealt pocket Nines might invest more money to see if things improve. If you were observant enough to have seen that one Nine was dealt and quickly folded, you can adjust your drawing expectations accordingly.

TIP

By fifth street you really need to have made a strong hand as the next three rounds will be at the higher limit. If your hand is still weak, throw it away. Never throw good money after bad.

Calling stations

With so much information available and the opportunity to improve a number of hands with each turn, Seven-card Stud generates a lot of action and a lot of players fall into the trap of calling too many bets. Don't do this – playing like a rock is the best tactic. Even if you wait for strong paired, connected or suited starting cards, you're still likely to find players willing to call your bets, so don't worry too much about your table image.

Table information

If you're out of a particular hand, don't lose your focus. Apart from the opportunity to learn something about your table partners, you can continue to train yourself in the art of accumulating information. Ultimately you want to tune your brain to the game to a degree whereby, with just a glance at the table, you have a strong mental snapshot of how many suits are already out there and what high cards have been dealt.

Playing pairs

The best starting hand in Seven-card Stud is three-of-a-kind, but a pair of Aces or Kings is also very strong, especially if they're hidden. You should bet strongly with them, but you have to accept that if they don't improve by the fifth card and there has been plenty of betting and raising, you probably

TIP

If you're dealt three cards to a flush, quickly check your opponents' door cards. If you're playing at a full table, there is a lot of information right there that can tell you if it's worth chasing. If you've got three spades and you can already see another two or three spades exposed, it's probably not worth drawing unless your cards also give you other options.

Table information

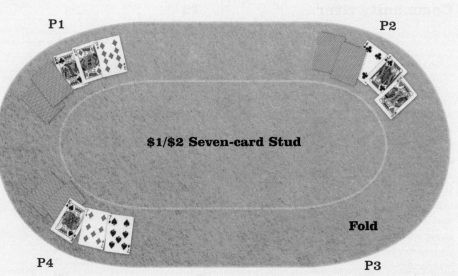

By fifth street each player has three cards exposed, so a wealth of information is already sitting at the table. Player 1 shows a pair of Kings, but as Kings are also visible in Player 2 and Player 3's hands, Player 1 won't be able to bluff (i.e. bet as if he had a concealed King for three of a kind).

P1

P2

$1/$2 Seven-card Stud

Fold

P4

P3

Advanced

Create an image. When you first sit at a table, only play solid hands. Showing down winning hands consistently will establish you as a quality player and earn you some respect. Later in the session you'll find you can exploit this position to win more hands without having to showdown so often. If you're playing pot or no-limit, such an image might also allow you to bully more people off pots with larger bets.

need to let them go. Easier said than done, but if you get to enough showdowns in Seven-card Stud with only a big pair, you'll soon understand the wisdom in this advice. This decision becomes easier should you see more of your outs appearing in other people's hands.

No-limit/Pot-limit

Though Seven-card Stud is traditionally a limit game, the popularity of no-limit and pot-limit games has meant that variations are now offered on most online sites, if not in poker rooms. The mechanics are essentially the same, with the same conditions controlling who starts the betting rounds, and what their minimum bets must be. Obviously, in the instance of pot or no-limit games, the ceiling on any betting round is no longer governed by the 'one bet, three raises' law. In pot-limit you can call the bet that's been posted before you and then raise the entire amount of the pot again. If the pot's $100 and the bet before you has been $20, you can add the $20 to the pot to call, and then raise an additional $120 to make the pot $240 in total. If you're playing no-limit you can raise and reraise as much as you want, and you can put all of your chips in the middle at any time. Certain conventions still govern no-limit games though – you can find detailed information in the dedicated Betting chapter later in the book.

WARNING!

If a full table of players stay in a hand right up until the river, there won't be enough cards to deal everyone their individual river cards. In this instance a final community card is dealt face-up on the table, and this can be used by everyone to complete their five-card poker hand.

Community river

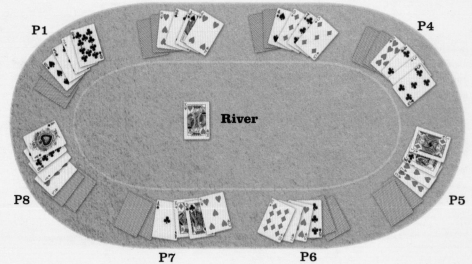

A full table of eight players means that 48 cards are already in use, and there aren't enough to deal the river. In this (admittedly rare) instance, one community river card is put on the table for all to use.

Starting hands

Being dealt three cards means that there are a variety of starting hands you can find yourself looking at, before any real betting has taken place. Here are the main groups these hands fall into, and some observations. Bear in mind that these tips are aimed at players in low-stake games playing relatively tight.

Connectors

You've got three connected cards and that qualifies as a strong hand as you have, at the very least, eight outs to complete a straight, and four cards still to come to you. Obviously, watching the initial door cards dealt to everyone can help you recalculate your odds on this. If two or more of the cards in your hand are suited, it improves your expectations, and the higher the cards, the better (for strong pair possibilities).

Combos

For a starting hand to be considered playable, it should contain a combination of cards that offer several types of outs. You don't want to lose a third of your potential hand at the start. The hand shown here could qualify as playable as it has concealed cards that could make high pairs, cards that could improve to a straight, and two suited cards that might improve to a reasonably high flush. If all three of your starting hands are high cards, chances are that if you catch a pair, it will be the best pair possible. This, of course, doesn't take into account any juicy concealed pocket pairs your opponents might have. Also, if the lowest card in your starting hand is higher than any card showing on the table you should be in pretty good shape.

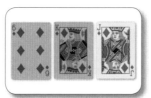

Flush up

If you get three starting cards of the same suit it's always worth playing them, unless there are already more than two cards of that suit already showing on the table. If your starting hand also contains high cards (that might improve to strong pairs or trips) or connected cards (that could ultimately form a straight), this should contribute to your decision whether to continue.

Trips

The strongest hand you can be dealt in Seven-card Stud is three-of-a-kind 'rolled-up'. However, you must still be super-aware of the cards that the other players are receiving. If your set is low it can easily be bust, and you should certainly be prepared to throw these cards away if there are lots of strong possible flushes and straights against you, coupled with aggressive betting and raising. A lot of people lose a lot of money when dealt rolled-up trips, simply because they can't let them go.

Shut the door

When you start a new session with new players, only play door Aces if you can raise them up. If not, then fold them – and be sure to do it slowly enough so that everyone registers that you've just dumped an Ace. Later in the session, you might find that you can win uncontested pots (from players who saw you throw away previous door Aces) when you do raise up in the same position. They'll be thinking, 'If he threw an Ace away before, and now he is raising with one, he must have a pair?'

Further strategies

Play with your mind on these six points and you'll be a winning Stud player.

• **The most important decision in Stud** is whether to continue beyond your initial deal. Financing the fourth card can still be expensive, even at this early stage in the hand. Only do it if you really believe you can win, and similarly be ready to dump the hand if the fourth card you pay for doesn't meet your expectations.

• **Beware exposed pairs.** If an opponent is playing a split pair in his starting hand (i.e. one concealed and one shown), and then goes on to pair his door card on fourth street, there's a strong possibility that he now holds trips.

• **Pay attention to the board for key cards** that affect your chances of completing a hand. A low pair is only worth playing if, in addition to the strength of it being a pair, it also has the potential to improve into trips. Playing 7-7 no longer makes sense if you know that both the other Sevens are already out of play (i.e. in the hands of others, or are already in the muck from folded players' hands).

• **Always be on the lookout for good reasons to fold.** It sounds silly but, if you look for good reasons to fold but can't find any, you're probably right to continue in the hand. Specifically look for dead cards or exposed cards that your current strategy relies on. You'll feel a lot more confident continuing in a hand once you've grilled yourself and come up smiling.

• **Watch your opponents,** as in any game of poker. If you dump your starting hand, you could have a fair period of time before the next hand begins, so make good use of it and watch your opponents. Because of the amount of cards moving around in Seven-card Stud, many beginners find it hard to keep track of all their cards and watch their opponents, so make use of the time you have when you aren't in a hand to accumulate as much information as possible.

• **Adapt to the environment.** If you find yourself among weak and passive players who tend to check until they hit a hand, take advantage. Even if it's not normally your style, bully those players silly enough to check to you in a late position. If you do get caught, you can use this as an opportunity to sow the seeds in everyone's heads that you're a wild, loose bluffer. If, however, everyone at your table appears to be a maniac – betting and raising every single pot – then sit back and ride out the storm. Each hand you fold will only cost you a small ante, and only winning one pot an hour will still leave you in profit. Don't feel you have to get involved with the crazy people unless you really want to.

Starting hand probabilities

Small Blind	%	Odds against being dealt	Number of possible combinations
3 x Aces	0.02	5,524-1	4
3 x Jacks thru Kings	0.05	1,841-1	12
3 x Sixes thru Tens	0.09	1,104-1	20
3 x Twos thru Fives	0.07	1,380-1	16
Pair Aces	1.30	75.7-1	288
Pair Jacks thru Kings	3.91	24.6-1	864
Pair Sixes thru Tens	6.52	14.3-1	1,440
Pair Twos thru Fives	5.21	18.2-1	1,152
Three cards to straight flush	1.16	85.3-1	256
Three cards to a flush	4.02	23.9-1	888
Three cards to straight	17.38	4.76-1	3,840
Any three of a kind	0.24	424-1	52
Any pair	16.94	4.90-1	3,744

Key points: 1) Rolled-up trips don't come along often, so maximize them when they do. Your opponents will also be aware of the odds against bumping into concealed trips from third street, so milk them for as much as you can. 2) Because of the combinations possible, being dealt three cards with straight possibilities is more common than receiving a pair. However, you MUST be able to dump these cards if they don't improve. Watch the other exposed cards on the table to evaluate your chances of completing a strong straight.

Stud variants

Seven-card Stud might be the most popular of the Stud games, but there are plenty of other variants you can play when you have mastered the basics.

Five-card Stud

Five-card Stud follows most of the rules you are now familiar with, but with only five cards. The sequence of play is obviously shorter, but the premise remains the same – some of your cards are concealed, but the majority are revealed.

Sequence of play

Following an ante posted by all the players, everyone receives one card face-down and one card face-up. The player with the lowest shown hand must bring-in and the following players must call, raise or fold. There is then a third face-up card dealt to all players, followed by a round of betting that must be initiated by the player showing the strongest hand. Should any players show the same hand, action must begin with the player nearest the dealer's left. A fourth card is dealt face-up to all players, followed by a fourth round of betting according to the standard rules. A fifth and final card is dealt face-up to all players, and a final round of betting takes place.

Seven-card Stud Hi-Lo

A very popular variant of Seven-card Stud is Hi-Lo. In Hi-Lo each pot is won by a high hand and any qualifying low hand. For a hand to qualify as low it must have five cards no higher than an eight. The pairs are played as both high and low, but straights

Five-card Stud

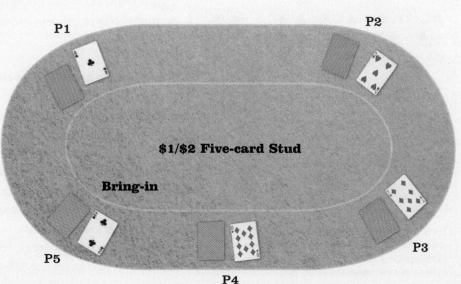

Stage 1
Each player is dealt one card face-down and one card face-up. If a bring-in is being used, the player with the lowest-value card starts the sequence. If not, then the highest card shown begins.

P1

P2

$1/$2 Five-card Stud

Bring-in

P5

P4

P3

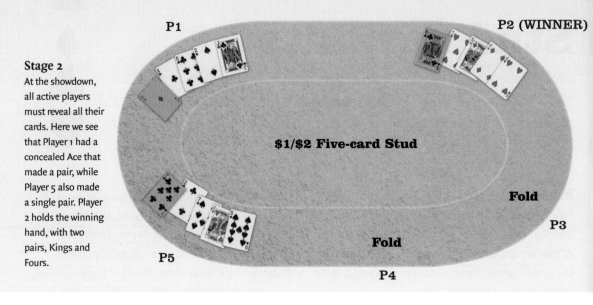

P1

P2 (WINNER)

Stage 2
At the showdown, all active players must reveal all their cards. Here we see that Player 1 had a concealed Ace that made a pair, while Player 5 also made a single pair. Player 2 holds the winning hand, with two pairs, Kings and Fours.

$1/$2 Five-card Stud

Fold

P3

Fold

P5

P4

and flushes do not disqualify a hand for low, so the best low hand would be A-2-3-4-5. Remembering that you'll make the best five-card hand from the seven you hold, it's feasible that a player with A-2-3-4-5 as a low hand could also win the high with 3-4-5-6-7 if those were the seven cards he held in total.

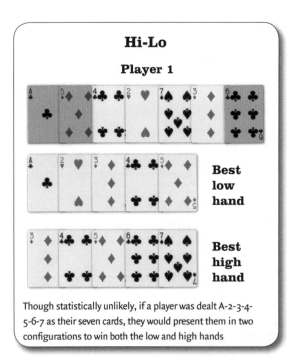

Hi-Lo

Player 1

Best low hand

Best high hand

Though statistically unlikely, if a player was dealt A-2-3-4-5-6-7 as their seven cards, they would present them in two configurations to win both the low and high hands

Hi-Lo strategy

The most important thing to bear in mind with Hi-Lo games is the huge difference between the profit made winning half the pot, and the profit made scooping the entire pot. Beginners tend to think that winning half a pot is worth paying for, but in truth you're not going to get much more than you put in. Good Hi-Lo players often have to settle for only half, and occasionally indeed nothing, but always play hands that at least have a good chance of taking the lot. It's very rarely worth fighting to only win one-half, unless you cannot be beaten.

Strong starting hands in Seven-card Stud Hi-Lo
- three-of-a-kind
- three low cards to a straight flush (e.g. 7s-4s-3s)
- three low cards to a straight (e.g. 6h-4s-2c)
- three low cards to a flush (e.g. 3c-6c-8c)
  Note: with the latter three starting hands you should check-fold if the hand doesn't improve on the next card drawn, and you're facing two or more better low hand draws.
- three low cards including an Ace (e.g. 8-4-A)
- a low pair plus an ace (e.g. 6-6-A)

Hi-Lo hand breakdown

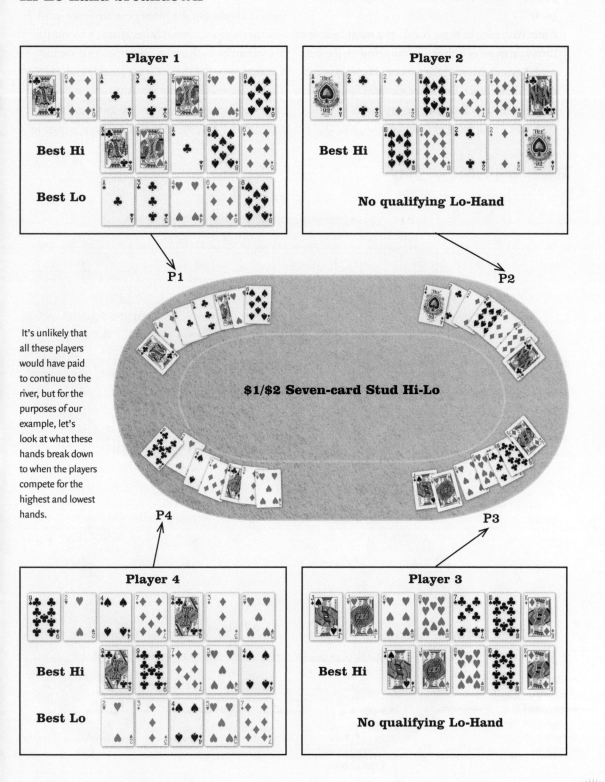

It's unlikely that all these players would have paid to continue to the river, but for the purposes of our example, let's look at what these hands break down to when the players compete for the highest and lowest hands.

$1/$2 Seven-card Stud Hi-Lo

- **pair of Nines or Tens with an Ace (e.g. 9-9-A, 10-10-A)**

  Note: With each of these hands you must be able to throw them away if they don't develop on the next card. Beyond this card the cost of playing goes up to the higher limit. Do not be tempted to cross your fingers and keep financing losing hands.
- **high pair – concealed or split (e.g. AA, KK, QQ)**

Razz

Razz is another of the more popular Seven-card Stud derivatives, probably because it's so similar in mechanics to the original game. This means that newcomers can pick it up quickly and easily. Razz is played in exactly the same way as Seven-card Stud, only with Ace-to-Five low hand values scoring. In Razz, the highest door card brings-in

Razz: sequence of play

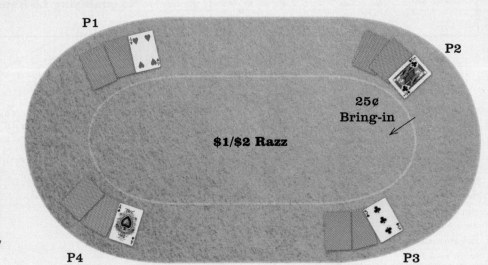

Stage 1
Player 2 has the highest card (Player 4's Ace is low in Razz) so Player 2 must pay the bring-in.

25¢ Bring-in

$1/$2 Razz

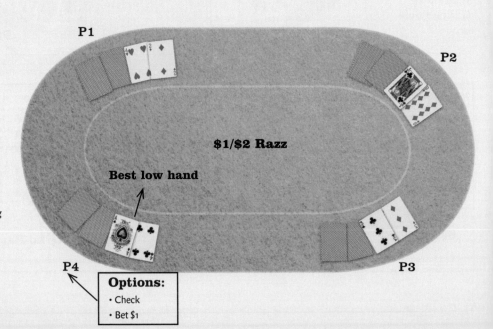

Stage 2
Player 4 is showing the lowest hand and initiates the next round of betting.

Best low hand

$1/$2 Razz

Options:
- Check
- Bet $1

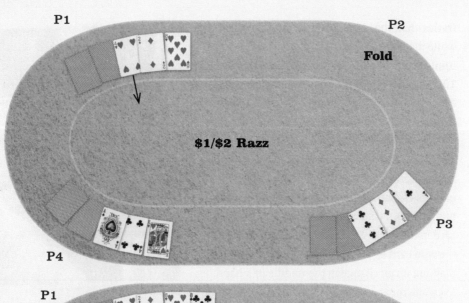

Stage 3

Because of the King arriving in Player 4's hand, Player 1 now has the lowest hand and starts the betting round. As this is fifth street, the betting increments are now at the higher level, as in Seven-card Stud.

Stage 4

The arrival of a second Eight means that Player 3 now has the lowest hand (pair Threes against pair Eights).

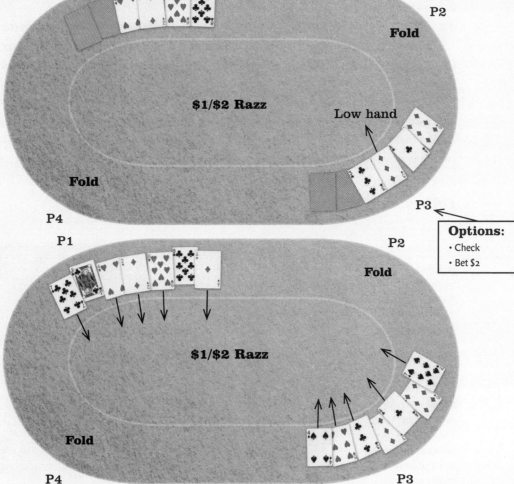

Options:
- Check
- Bet $2

Stage 5

Once the final down-card is dealt – followed by a last round of betting – the remaining players showdown to establish who has the lowest hand. Here P2 wins with a Seven as his highest card.

(rather than the lowest, as with Seven-card Stud), while the betting on the second and subsequent rounds is initiated by the lowest hand exposed. The best five-card hand possible in Razz is A-2-3-4-6. Note: Ace is always low in Razz.

Follow the Queen

There are lots of fun poker variants you can play at your home games, like Follow the Queen. This game is essentially the same as Seven-card Stud, but features a wild card, which can count as any card in the deck. The interesting thing is that the wild card is not defined until the game is in play and it can change in the middle of a hand. Everyone must wait until a Queen has been dealt face-up to a player during play. The next card dealt out will become the wild card.

A highly educational Razz mag

The bad news (for the player following the first Queen) is, should another Queen arrive at any point, then the card following that Queen now becomes the wild card and nullifies the previous wild card. This could seriously muck up any betting that was induced with the first wild card (which is why you're unlikely to see this as a high-stakes game at your casino in the near future). And, for one final twist, if the very last up-card dealt in the game is a Queen, all the wild cards are cancelled and you play the game as a standard Seven-card Stud hand. This is tremendous fun as a social game as people's hand values are changing all the time. If there was ever a game to test people's poker faces, Follow the Queen is it!

Follow the Queen

With the first card of fourth street being dealt to Player 2, the Queen has arrived! The next card will be defined as the wild card. Player 3 is the next to receive a card, and gets a Six. Sixes are now wild cards for the rest of that hand. This is also great news to Player 1 and anyone with a Six concealed in their hand!

P1

P2

Queen arrives

Wild

$1/$2 Follow the Queen

P4

P3

Checklist

- You can still find Seven-card Stud in live and online poker rooms
- But it's probably the most complicated poker variant you can play
- Giving the game your full attention is the only way to succeed
- So you'd better have a good memory
- Being able to lay down hands is the most important ability
- Having some strict starting hand criteria will save you money in the long run
- Follow the Queen is great fun to play at home

Can you remember how many suits were exposed on the table?

Draw

'Is that the game where one receives five cards? And if there's two alike that's pretty good, but if there's three alike, that's much better?'
W. C. FIELDS

In this chapter you'll learn...

Draw poker is the one you played when you were a kid. It's considered the most basic form and the one from which all other variants are derived, but there's much more to this deceptively simple game than meets the eye...

Paul Newman looking worried in *The Sting*

Five-card Draw

Draw poker is one of the oldest and most basic of all the poker variants you can play, which makes it an ideal place to start if you're a total beginner.

That's not to say that Draw poker is easy to master – play it at a decent level and there are lots of strategic implications. At heart though it's extremely basic and uncomplicated. Unlike other poker games you get dealt your five cards at the start. All you have to do is choose which cards you want to discard and change. Different types of Draw allow for a different number of discard rounds during the course of a hand, as well as the number of cards that you can change.

Sequence of play

Before you start you need to decide on a dealer. This is normally done by dealing everyone at the table a card, with the high card taking the button. As you take it in turn to discard (starting with the person to the left of the dealer), the dealer has to replenish each hand so that everyone is holding five cards at all times. After each hand, the dealer button moves round one place clockwise.

Five-card Draw is a great place to learn the basics of poker

Antes and blinds

These are forced bets that have to be placed before the cards are dealt. Antes – a set amount of money that ALL players have to post – are often used in home games. Blinds are more usual in casinos and online games, with the player sitting to the left of the dealer posting the small blind, and the player to their left posting the big blind. These forced bets kick-start the action in the first betting round.

The deal

Working clockwise from the dealer (starting with the player to his immediate left), each player receives a single card, working round the table continuously until everyone is holding five cards. All these cards are dealt face-down and, unlike

Antes and blinds

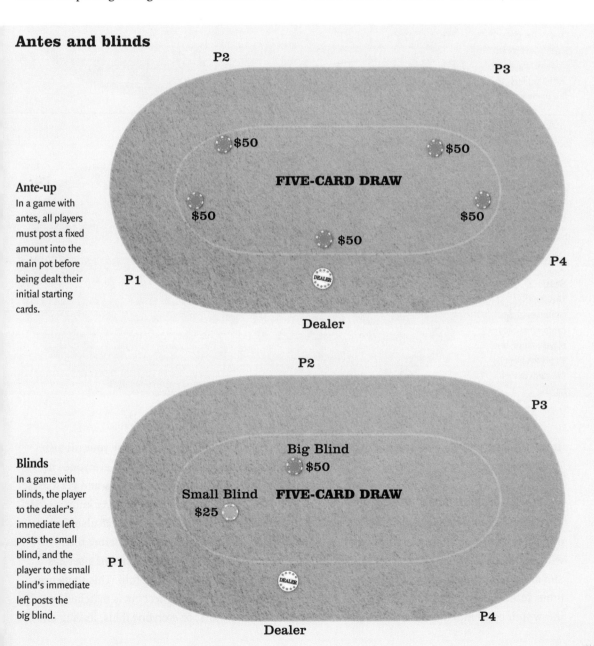

Ante-up
In a game with antes, all players must post a fixed amount into the main pot before being dealt their initial starting cards.

Blinds
In a game with blinds, the player to the dealer's immediate left posts the small blind, and the player to the small blind's immediate left posts the big blind.

The Deal

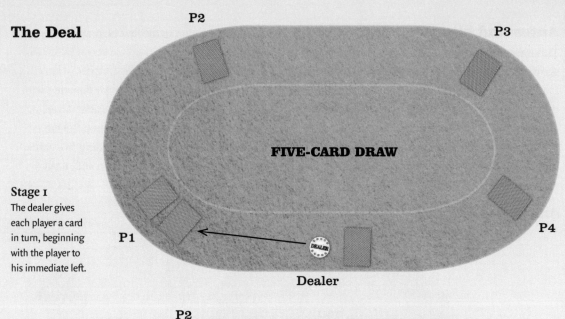

FIVE-CARD DRAW

Stage 1
The dealer gives each player a card in turn, beginning with the player to his immediate left.

P2

P3

P1

P4

Dealer

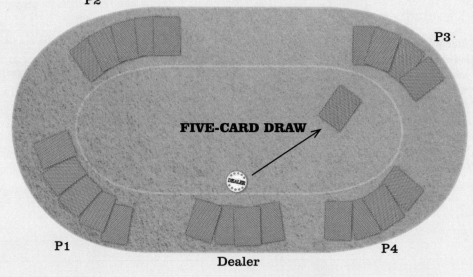

FIVE-CARD DRAW

Stage 2
The dealer continues to deal cards out to each player in turn, until all players have five cards in their hands.

P2

P3

P1

P4

Dealer

Texas Hold'em, there are no community cards. What you see is what you've got.

Betting in an ante game

The action begins with the player to the left of the dealer, who can either check (indicating a pass with no bet made) or bet between the minimum and maximum amount allowed by the game's limit. Technically you can also choose to fold and throw your cards into the muck at this point, but

you're better off checking in case your rubbish cards become a winning hand. If everyone checks, you could throw all five cards away and get a royal flush. Highly unlikely, but you never know.

Players following in sequence can also then check (if there has been no bet before them), bet, call (matching the bet), raise (if a bet has been made before them) or fold. This sequence continues until the highest bet is matched by all active players, or everyone folds, leaving one player who takes the pot. Once every player has completed this round of betting, the chips are gathered into the pot and you start discarding.

Betting in a blinded game

When blinds are in play, the first round of betting begins with the player to the left of the big blind. This player must call (i.e. match) the big blind to continue in the hand, or make a raise between the minimum and maximum amount allowed, or fold. Subsequent players must either match the bet before them, raise or fold. This sequence continues until all players have matched the highest bet or folded, at which point all the chips are gathered into the pot and you move to the discard period.

Discarding

Once the initial round of betting has been completed, you have the option to discard any of the cards in your current hand, and replace them with new cards from the deck – starting with the player to the left of the dealer. Some variations on the game limit the number of cards that can be exchanged, but you can usually swap as many or as few as you like. Next, you pass your discards to the dealer, face-down. The number of cards you're exchanging must be clearly stated so that everyone can hear. The dealer then replaces the number of cards you've discarded with an equal number – again delivered face-down – leaving you with five cards in your hand. This process moves clockwise around the table, and the last person to act is the dealer.

Stand pat

You can also announce that you're standing pat, which means that you're happy with the five cards you've got and don't want to discard or receive any new ones. This happens for one of two reasons. You might have been dealt a good hand (e.g. a straight), or you've decided that you're going to try to win the pot by bluffing – trying to convince the other players round the table that

your hand is so strong that you don't need to improve.

If you sense weakness in your opponents when you have been dealt an almost unplayable pile of junk, you can make a strong raise, followed by standing pat, which can mislead your opponents into believing you have been dealt a good hand.

In the example on the following page, starting the action from the position behind the big blind, Player 3 folds and Player 4 calls. You then raise, indicating a strong hand to your opponents. Player 1 and Player 2 call the remainder to match your raise, and Player 4 reconsiders his hand before opting to fold. Player 1 exchanges three cards, indicating that he's currently holding a pair. Player 2 also exchanges three cards. Though you've got precisely nothing of any note, you opt to stand pat. This – in conjunction with the raise you made in the first round of betting – should mislead your opponents into believing that not only was your hand strong enough to make a raise pre-discard, but it is already a 'made' hand that needs no further improvement. Players 1 and 2 check to you and you make a bet, confirming their worst fears. They both fold and you win the pot with the worst hand on the table.

It proves you don't necessarily need to hold the

///////////////////////////

WARNING!

Standing pat should only be attempted in optimum situations as it's an extremely dangerous move that can easily backfire. You can turn a dead hand into a winning one, but it's vital that you do it at the right time and in the right situation. If you run into an opposing monster hand you're in big trouble, and if you try the move too often people will rumble you. An ideal time is when you're in a late betting position (i.e. on or close to the button), when all the players who have acted before you have shown weakness with discards that suggest their hands are far from made. Even this isn't a cast-iron guarantee though; you bluff at your own risk.

///////////////////////////

Stand pat

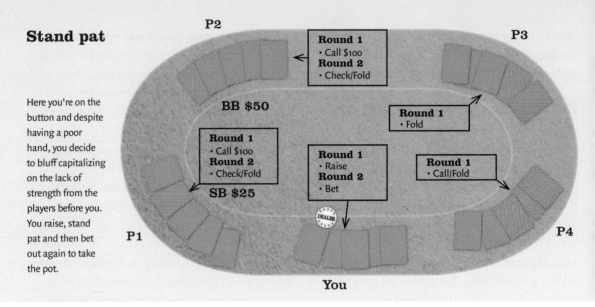

Here you're on the button and despite having a poor hand, you decide to bluff capitalizing on the lack of strength from the players before you. You raise, stand pat and then bet out again to take the pot.

P2

Round 1
• Call $100
Round 2
• Check/Fold

BB $50

P3

Round 1
• Fold

Round 1
• Call $100
Round 2
• Check/Fold

SB $25

Round 1
• Raise
Round 2
• Bet

Round 1
• Call/Fold

P1

DEALER

P4

You

winning hand in poker, you just need to be able to make a winning move.

Final betting round

Most draw games have only two betting rounds – the first after the initial deal, and the second after the discard and replacement of your cards. Once everyone at the table has received their replacement cards, the action falls again to the player immediately to the dealer's left, who must

check, bet or fold. Play continues around the table until all betting has been completed.

Showdown

If only one player remains active by the end of the final betting round (i.e. all players have folded to one single player's bet) then that one remaining player wins the entire pot, and is not obliged to show the hand (it's entirely discretionary – do if you want but be aware that

Showdown

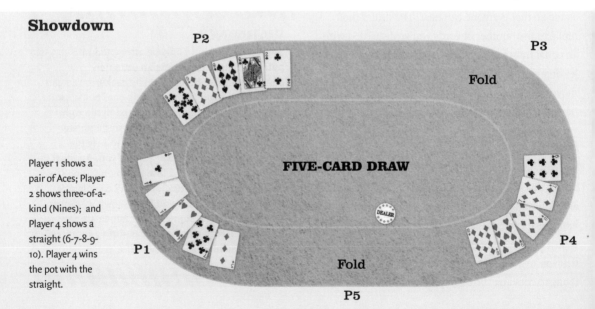

Player 1 shows a pair of Aces; Player 2 shows three-of-a-kind (Nines); and Player 4 shows a straight (6-7-8-9-10). Player 4 wins the pot with the straight.

P2

P3

Fold

FIVE-CARD DRAW

DEALER

P1

P4

Fold

P5

you're giving away free information).

If there's more than one player left in at the end of the final betting round, all active players show their hands and a winner is declared as per the usual poker five-card rankings (see page 14).

If two players hold exactly the same hand, the pot is split.

Common mistakes

It might seem like a basic game, but there's still

TIP

You can never be completely sure what your opponents are holding unless you pay to make them honest and take them to the showdown, but you can gather a lot of information from the number of cards they choose to discard.

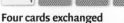

Five cards exchanged
A sure-fire guarantee that the hand was woeful. It's not impossible that the replacement hand could be quite reasonable, but it's extremely unlikely. If someone is left in the game with nothing in their hand it suggests that the prior betting has been particularly timid – any sort of bet or raise should have forced them to throw in their cards.

Four cards exchanged
Not much better than a five-card exchange, although keeping hold of one indicates a high card, probably an Ace. Someone who draws four cards is only going to cause you trouble if they get very lucky with their replacements.

Three cards exchanged
A good indication that they've picked up a pair and are hoping to improve to two-pair or trips. It's very unlikely that they're aiming for a flush or a straight – miracles do happen, but at best you should only worry about them possibly holding three-of-a-kind or two pairs after the exchange.

Two cards exchanged
This is the hardest one to interpret as there are so many possibilities. They could already be holding three-of-a-kind, as well as aiming for a straight or a flush. Watch their betting after the redraw. If they bet aggressively, chances are they started with trips, or have managed to improve their hand. Weak betting after exchanging three cards suggests a weak hand.

One card exchanged
Suggests they could have been dealt two pairs and are looking for a matching card to complete a full house. More often, though, this indicates aiming for a straight or a flush, with a single card needed to make the hand. Watch how they bet after the discard and be wary of signs of super strength. If they were drawing there's no guarantee they've hit.

TIP

Look at the poker hand rankings on page 14. The odds of getting dealt those five cards applies precisely to Draw and, as you can see, the chances of your getting dealt a royal flush are astronomical. You can use these odds to judge how strong your hand is. If you've got a pair, you can bet that at 5-2 a couple of other people around the table will have them as well – hopefully yours will be higher. If you've been dealt two-pair or above, the chances are you're currently in the lead. Get dealt a royal flush and you've hit the jackpot.

plenty of strategy involved in Draw and a lot of potential mistakes to be avoided, like...

• Constantly limping in

If you're dealt a hand that is clearly weak or one which will only improve to a winning hand with a 'miracle' draw, don't stay in the game with your fingers crossed. It's a sure-fire way to lose money quickly. This is even more important when you are playing with a full table of players, or when you're sitting in an early position. If your hand is not good enough to raise here, don't play it.

• Calling bets when clearly beaten

Be ready to let your hand go. Don't throw good money after bad on a hunch, or because you feel you have invested so much money in the pot that you've got to continue to the end. Against the very few times that you'll catch a bluffer playing weak cards, you will more often run into a player with a stronger hand than yours. Know when you are losing, and act accordingly – fold.

• Strength relative to position

A pair of Eights in your starting hand may be playable in a late position, but should be avoided in an early position where lots of action behind you could make your involvement expensive.

Playing position:
• Early

With a pair of Eights you only want to limp in if possible and improve with a draw of three

Playing position

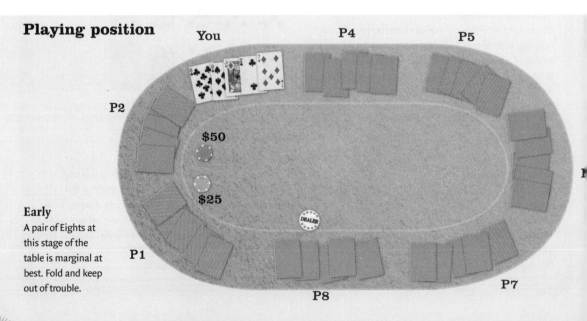

Early
A pair of Eights at this stage of the table is marginal at best. Fold and keep out of trouble.

cards. With so many players behind you, the chances of getting in cheaply are remote. This will either waste the money it costs you to call, or put pressure on you to call an expensive raise. Save yourself the trouble and fold.

• Later

In a much later table position, you're more likely to get away with limping into the pot without a subsequent raise. You're also in a stronger position following the discard as you're the last to act. Even if you don't improve your hand, you might decide to bluff at the pot if players before you show weakness. If you do improve (for example, to two-pair, three-of-a-kind, full house or quads) then you're in the best position to maximize your winnings on this hand.

Drawing to straights and flushes

Apart from single pairs, the most common hands you'll get from your initial deal are straight draws and flush draws. But a very common mistake is to invest too much in them. On a full table, you can easily assume that at least one person's

Advanced!
Drawing is a risky business, even when you just need a single card to hit your hand. Got four clubs and need one to make your flush? You're drawing to a 4-1 shot. Got two pair and looking for a full house? You're drawing to an approximate 11-1 shot. Inside straight and open-ended straight draws are approximately 11-1 and 5-1 respectively. By all means draw to these hands, but don't expect to hit them all the time, and make sure you're getting correct value from the pot in relation to the money you're putting in.

sitting on a pair, which means you're drawing from a losing position. For this reason, you shouldn't bet hoping for a miracle draw, or play draws in an early position and/or against large raises. You can never justify – and this maxim applies to any game of poker – putting large amounts of money into the pot where you are crossing your fingers and praying. Once you've drawn to too many hopeful straights and flushes without ever completing them, you'll drop the habit. Try not picking it up in the first place. It can prove to be an extremely expensive and frustrating lesson to learn the hard way.

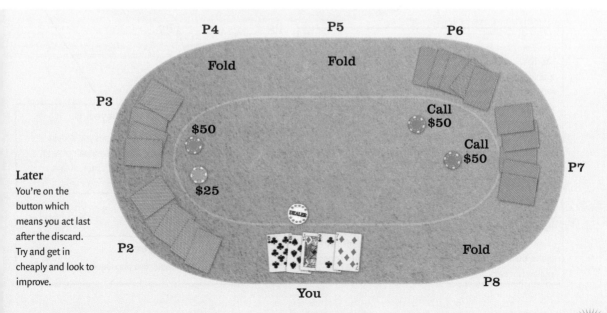

P4 **P5** **P6**

Fold Fold

P3

$50 Call $50

Call $50

$25 **P7**

Later
You're on the button which means you act last after the discard. Try and get in cheaply and look to improve.

P2

Fold

P8

You

Starting pairs – eight-handed

In any draw game with a full table of eight players, you need to be very selective about the starting pairs you play relevant to your position. If the player to the left of the dealer is Player 1, and the player to their left is Player 2, etc., here are some possible hands for each position. Remember that there is a small and big blind in effect, so the play actually begins with Player 3.

Positional pairs

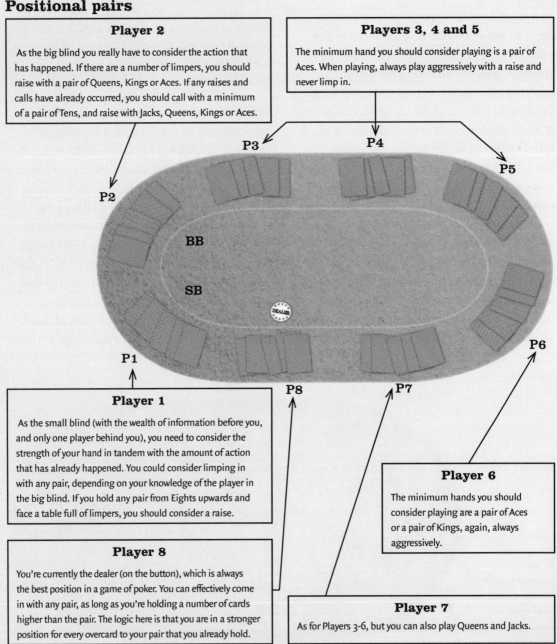

Player 2

As the big blind you really have to consider the action that has happened. If there are a number of limpers, you should raise with a pair of Queens, Kings or Aces. If any raises and calls have already occurred, you should call with a minimum of a pair of Tens, and raise with Jacks, Queens, Kings or Aces.

Players 3, 4 and 5

The minimum hand you should consider playing is a pair of Aces. When playing, always play aggressively with a raise and never limp in.

Player 1

As the small blind (with the wealth of information before you, and only one player behind you), you need to consider the strength of your hand in tandem with the amount of action that has already happened. You could consider limping in with any pair, depending on your knowledge of the player in the big blind. If you hold any pair from Eights upwards and face a table full of limpers, you should consider a raise.

Player 6

The minimum hands you should consider playing are a pair of Aces or a pair of Kings, again, always aggressively.

Player 8

You're currently the dealer (on the button), which is always the best position in a game of poker. You can effectively come in with any pair, as long as you're holding a number of cards higher than the pair. The logic here is that you are in a stronger position for every overcard to your pair that you already hold.

Player 7

As for Players 3-6, but you can also play Queens and Jacks.

Triple Draw

You're not always looking for the high cards in poker. In Triple Draw, the lower your cards the better.

In recent years Draw has been completely overshadowed by Texas Hold'em and Seven-card Stud, but Triple Draw is starting to worm its way back into people's affections, especially among poker aficionados who play it for dizzying stakes in the casinos in Las Vegas. Basically, Triple Draw is Five-card Draw where the lowest hand wins and, as the name suggests, you get three opportunities to change your cards. This means Triple Draw contains four betting rounds, as opposed to Five-card Draw's two.

The most common variation is Triple Draw Deuce to Seven where pairs, flushes and straights still count as per the hand rankings but aren't as welcome. You want to make the lowest hand possible (note that Aces are high) so a royal flush is the very worst hand you can possibly get. The very best hand in Triple Draw Deuce to Seven is 2-3-4-5-7 (not 2-3-4-5-6, which would make a straight). Because you've got three opportunities to improve your hand, you're unlikely to win it when you're holding a high pair.

You can alternatively play A-5 Triple Draw, where Aces are low and straights and flushes don't count. The best possible hand here is A-2-3-4-5.

Checklist

- **Draw is an extremely simple poker variant**
- **There are no community cards**
- **You get all five cards at the start**
- **And discard and draw new ones to improve your hand**
- **In most games of Draw you can choose to discard any number of cards**
- **Or you can stand pat with a really bad hand...**
- **And hope you don't get called by a monster**
- **A royal flush is the worst hand you can make in Triple Draw**

Betting

5

'One of these days in your travels, a guy is going to come up to you and show you a nice brand-new deck of cards on which the seal is not yet broken, and this guy is going to offer to bet you that he can make the Jack of spades jump out of the deck and squirt cider in your ear. But, son, do not bet this man, for as sure as you are standing there, you are going to end up with an earful of cider.'

DAMON RUNYON

In this chapter you'll learn...

Betting is the most powerful weapon in your armoury, even more so than the cards. A good bet asks questions, demands answers and puts pressure on your opponents. Learning how to put chips properly in the middle of the table means that you'll end up taking many more out. And that's the aim of the game.

California Split: learn to bet properly or risk the wrath of your fellow players

Betting

It's said that poker takes minutes to learn and a lifetime to master, and it's the same with betting. There aren't that many moves you can actually make but you can use them in a million different ways.

You might think that poker's a card game but it's actually more of a gambling game where the cards are used to manufacture the odds and create the situations for you to wager on. Learn how to bet properly and you'll be an infinitely better poker player.

Blinds and antes

These are forced bets that are made before any cards are dealt, ensuring that there's always something to play for. If you're playing a game with blinds, the two players to the left of the dealer post the small and big blinds respectively. The first of the two is the small blind, and the second – usually twice the amount – the big blind. They count as active bets. Then, after the cards are dealt, the betting starts with the player

You can live without good cards but, if you can't bet like a pro, you're dead in the water

to the left of the big blind who must match the bet to stay in the hand. In all the other betting rounds, the action starts with the player to the immediate left of the dealer (the small blind). This person is said to be under the gun.

Antes are small, forced bets that are placed by every player at the table before any cards are dealt, and sometimes antes are used in conjunction with blinds to create a bigger starting pot.

Your betting moves
Check

Checking allows you to stay in the hand without making a bet, but you can only do this when there's been no bet or raise before you. This happens when you're the first to bet in a round with no blinds, or when you're following on from players who have checked before you. You can check to try and improve a hand without spending any more money. Or you can be extra cunning and use it to disguise a monster hand in a bid to trap your opponents.

TIP

In live games, you can indicate a check by simply tapping on the table. Be careful not to tap on the table when it's your turn to act if you don't want to check. Even if you were just tapping along to your MP3 player, if the dealer clocks it he'll take it as your intended action and move to the next player.

This is where you want to be depositing your chips at the end of the night

Bet

If you are the first to act in a round of betting, or all the other players before you have checked, you can choose to be the aggressor and bet. The amount you can bet is determined by the type of game that you're playing. In limit games you have to bet at either the lower or higher limits as dictated by the level of the game. If you're playing no-limit, you can move all your chips into the middle whenever you feel like it. See page 75 for more on the different types of game you can play and how they affect your betting.

Call

If there's been a bet before you and you want to stay in the hand, you have to at least call the bet. Calling a bet simply means matching the bet placed before you.

Raising

Raising a pot means making a larger bet than the one that has been made before you. As with betting, the amount you can raise is dependent on the type of game you're playing. If you choose to raise the pot, everyone left to act after you has to match your raise, or reraise you to stay in the pot.

Reraise

If someone raises before you, you can choose to reraise the bet – normally the sign of a monster hand or a stone-cold bluff. Either way it's a power move. If someone reraises you significantly be prepared to go all the way with your hand if you decide to call. As before, the amount you can reraise depends on the type of game you're playing.

WARNING!

One of the mistakes made impossible by Internet poker is betting out of turn. So when you come to play your first live game, wait until you are 100 per cent sure it's your turn to act before you check, fold or bet. Consistently acting out of turn will make you extremely unpopular.

Check-raise

Check-raising used to be seen as a sneaky, underhand move. Some card rooms even had rulings preventing you from doing it which is, of course, ridiculous. In today's aggressive poker scene, check-raising is not only an accepted part of the game, but an extremely powerful weapon.

To check-raise is to opt to check when the action is on you, but to then make a raise on top of any of the bets that follow. Be wary of getting caught in the check-raise trap yourself. If someone checks into you, you might register this as a sign of weakness and bet in an attempt to steal the pot. But if the player who checks comes back at you with a raise, what are you going to do? Beware of donating large chunks of your chip stack to check-raising players unless you have a strong hand yourself.

Straddle bets

You won't find straddle bets online, but you might well come across them in live poker. A straddle bet is essentially a voluntary third blind that acts as a blind raise; and as it's counted as a third blind the person who makes a straddle bet is allowed to raise the pot when the action comes back round to him. As the person who places the straddle hasn't seen his cards it's very hard to know how to react to a straddle bet. If he gets weak cards he can bluff more effectively, and if he's lucky enough to get a premium hand, he might be able to draw more money out of an unsuspecting opponent.

Say what you mean

Harking back to the fact that it's very hard to make human errors in an online game (i.e. acting out of turn, betting the wrong amount, and folding live cards, etc.), one of the

Straddle bets

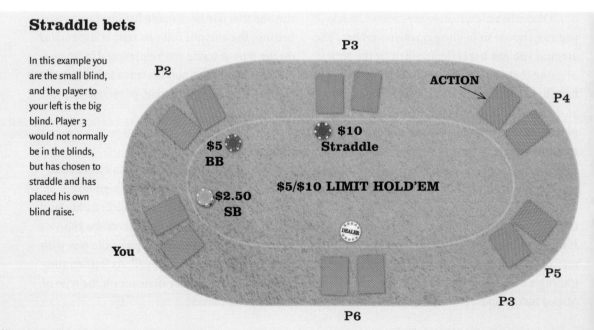

In this example you are the small blind, and the player to your left is the big blind. Player 3 would not normally be in the blinds, but has chosen to straddle and has placed his own blind raise.

P3

P2

ACTION

P4

$10
Straddle

$5
BB

$5/$10 LIMIT HOLD'EM

$2.50
SB

DEALER

You

P5

P3

P6

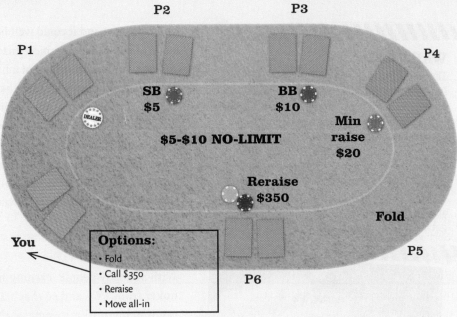

No-limit

Here, Player 4 is the first to act and makes the minimum raise to $20. Player 5 folds and Player 6 opts to make a reraise. The reraise must be at least double the previous bet (in this case it would need to be at least another $20) but Player 6 chooses to make the bet $350. You can fold, call the $350 bet or reraise no less than an additional $350, or up to your entire chip stack.

P2

P3

P1

P4

SB $5

BB $10

Min raise $20

$5-$10 NO-LIMIT

Reraise $350

Fold

DEALER

You

P5

Options:
- Fold
- Call $350
- Reraise
- Move all-in

P6

simplest ways to avoid ever having your actions misinterpreted in real-life is to state exactly what you plan to do in all betting situations. If you plan to raise another 100 into the pot, tell the players and dealers, 'raise another 100'. If you are raising a pot of 100 up to 300, then say 'make it 300 in total'. You can describe your bid however you want, so long as it's completely unambiguous. And remember that a verbal declaration is binding – once you've stated your intention you must do it.

How much can you bet?

The type of poker you're playing dictates the amount that you can bet at any one time, and this has a dramatic impact on the game. There are three variants: no-limit, limit (or fixed-limit) and pot-limit, and the differences in the betting are dramatic.

No-limit

If you're watching poker on TV, the chances are it'll be no-limit. No-limit games have set blinds (forced bets), but all other betting is uncapped, which means you can bet any amount of chips at any time, as long as you meet the minimum required to keep you in the hand. Sliding all your chips into the middle (called going all-in) is a powerful move that can win you a lot of pots. It's also a very risky manoeuvre – lose the hand and you stand to lose everything you've got.

The amounts stated in no-limit games are the small and big blinds. So, in a $5/$10 no-limit game, the small blind is $5, the big blind $10 and there's a minimum bet of $10 for each and every betting round. Generally, any raise has to be at least double the previous bet.

All-in

No matter what game you're playing, there'll come a time when you have to slide all of your remaining chips into the middle of the table (which obviously happens a lot more in no-limit games). This is called moving all-in, and it's one of the most dramatic and exciting moves you can make in the game. If you've got enough chips it's also devastatingly aggressive.

That's not always the case though. Find yourself

WARNING!

The string bet is one of the commonest mistakes in poker, and the cause of most arguments around the table. It occurs when you make a bet in stages, rather than in one fluid motion. So, if you want to raise a $5 bet by an additional $20, you must move all $20 of your chips forward at the same time. You can't put $10 forward and then go back to your stack for another $10. This is to avoid people declaring a raise, and then slowly adding more and more chips to the bet until they get a reaction from an opponent.

short-stacked and it could well be your only hope of survival. A common misconception is that you can get raised out of a hand of poker if an opponent bets more chips than you have left. This is pure bunkum – it certainly wouldn't make for a very interesting game. Instead, you can move all-in. The other players left in the hand can continue to bet, creating what's known as a side pot. You can only win the amount in the main pot, and can never win more from any one person than you put into the pot.

Limit

With so many people learning how to play poker from TV – and so much TV showing nothing but no-limit games – the betting sequence in limit games can seem confusing at first. It's actually extremely easy once you know the conventions. (And remember that if you're still unsure after reading this chapter you can watch Internet limit games whenever you want. Check the limits before you start playing and watch the betting patterns – all will become clear after a few rounds.)

Side pots

Here you've gone all-in pre-flop with your remaining $100. You are called by the three other players, forming a main pot of $400. You can win this at the end, but not the side pot which is created by the other players continuing to bet.

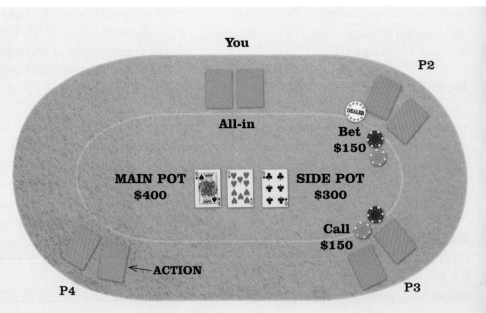

You

P2

All-in

Bet
$150

MAIN POT
$400

SIDE POT
$300

Call
$150

← ACTION

P4

P3

A limit game is defined by two amounts, for example $5/$10. These amounts refer to the two different stages of the betting. The smaller of the limits – $5 – refers to the amount you can bet before the flop and after the flop, and any raises have to be in $5 increments. The $10 refers to the betting after the turn (or fourth card) and the fiver (or fifth card).

The lower limit is also the amount of the big blind, and the small blind is half this. So in a $5/$10 game, the blinds are $2.50 and $5.00 respectively. This sets the action for the first bet of $5. (This is an important point to remember and this differs from no-limit games where the two stated amounts are the small and big blinds.)

Limit

Blinds

This is a fixed-limit $5/$10 game. The small blind is $2.50 and the big blind $5. Betting before and after the flop is made in $5 increments, and betting on the turn and the river is in increments of $10.

Pre-flop betting

With the blinds paid, all players receive their cards. Player 4 is first to act and has opted to call the big blind for $5. Player 5 has opted to raise, and adds an additional $5 to make the bet $10. You can opt to fold, call the $10 bet, or raise a further $5 to make a total bet of $15.

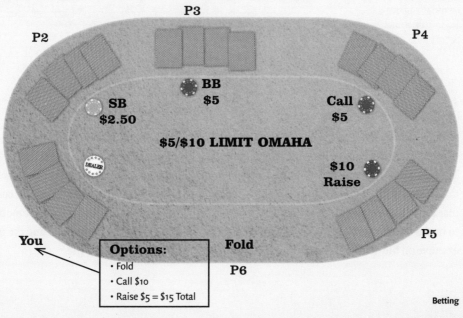

Options:
• Fold
• Call $10
• Raise $5 = $15 Total

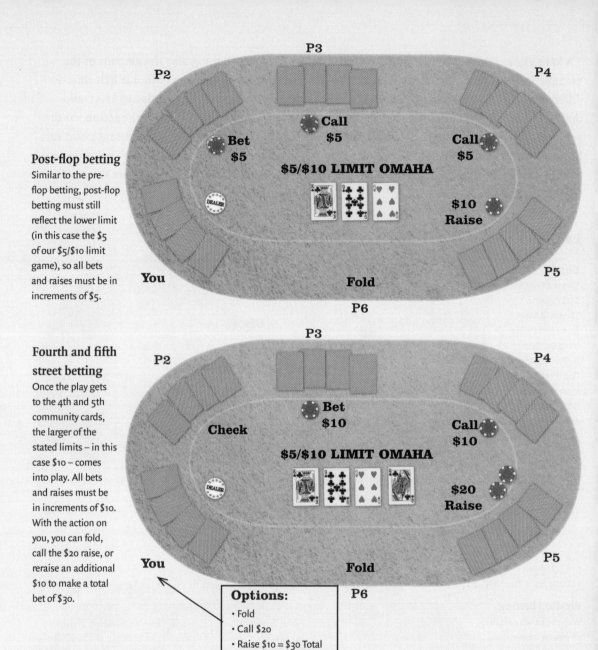

Post-flop betting

Similar to the pre-flop betting, post-flop betting must still reflect the lower limit (in this case the $5 of our $5/$10 limit game), so all bets and raises must be in increments of $5.

P3

P2

P4

Call $5

Bet $5

Call $5

$5/$10 LIMIT OMAHA

DEALER

$10 Raise

You

Fold

P5

P6

Fourth and fifth street betting

Once the play gets to the 4th and 5th community cards, the larger of the stated limits – in this case $10 – comes into play. All bets and raises must be in increments of $10. With the action on you, you can fold, call the $20 raise, or reraise an additional $10 to make a total bet of $30.

P3

P2

P4

Bet $10

Check

Call $10

$5/$10 LIMIT OMAHA

DEALER

$20 Raise

You

Fold

P5

P6

Options:
- Fold
- Call $20
- Raise $10 = $30 Total

Capping

In limit games there's normally a cap on the number of raises that can be made in a single betting round. The standard rule is one bet and three raises before the action is capped and no further raises can be made. At this point, any remaining players have to match the last bet if they want to stay in. In the example on the next page the betting is capped after three raises and your only option is to match the bet or fold your hand. The limits and the capping rule mean that the money staked on each hand in a limit game is much more controlled than in a no-limit game. This can also mean that more people stay in the hand until the end, raising the quality of hand needed to take the pot.

Capping

In this example, Player 3 is the first to bet. Players 4, 5 and 6 all opt to raise, making incremental bets as dictated by the limits. Player 6 has made the third raise, which means the betting is now capped and no further raises can be made. This means that your only options are to call the bet or fold your hand.

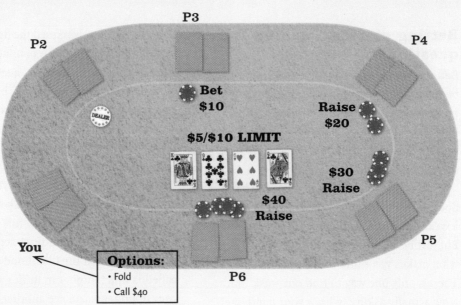

P3

P2

P4

Bet $10

Raise $20

$5/$10 LIMIT

$30 Raise

$40 Raise

P5

You

Options:
· Fold
· Call $40

P6

TIP

Bluffing is much more prevalent in no-limit and pot-limit games, where you can make huge bets in order to dissuade anyone else from calling unless they've got a very good hand. In limit games, where the betting is fixed, you'll find a lot more people calling the bet in order to improve their hands, so bluff with extreme caution.

Pot-limit

There is a middle ground between limit and no-limit games. Pot-limit games allow you some of the bullying moves of no-limit poker (there's nothing scarier than an opponent pushing a tower of chips towards you!), but with some control over the amount that you can bet. You can play any game of poker as a pot-limit game but some variations – like Omaha – are played almost exclusively as pot-limit.

Very simply, the maximum you can ever bet in a pot-limit game is dictated by the size of the pot. So if previous betting rounds have created a pot of $150, your opening bet must be no less than the big blind, and no more than the pot total.

As with no-limit games, the limits stated show you the small blind and the big blind. So in a $5/$10 game, the small blind is $5 and the big blind is $10. Each round begins with a minimum bet governed by the big blind. If you want to raise, the maximum allowed is the amount it takes you to call the bet before you *plus* the subsequent pot total.

And this is where the confusion normally occurs in pot-limit games – what is the exact amount you can raise? As the name suggests you're limited to the size of the pot, but a pot raise includes the amount you'd have to add to call any previous bet. So, in the example on the next page, the bet is $35 when it gets round to you. You can call the previous bet ($35) and then raise up to the amount of the entire pot ($85), making a total of $120.

If you're playing in a live game and you're unsure what the last bet was and the size of the pot, just ask. And if you want to make a pot-sized raise, just announce it clearly – 'I raise the pot' – and the dealer will work out how many chips you need to slide in. They're not just there to destroy your hands on the river.

Betting strategy: asking the question

Betting is often exclusively mistaken by beginners as a way of making money. You put money in the pot, and win or lose. Wrong. Betting is also the single most effective way of finding out what cards your opponents have got in their hands.

Just because you don't hold a strong hand doesn't mean you can't win the pot. If you hold a weak hand and don't bet, you will *never* win. But just because you haven't got a good hand, what makes you think your opponent has? There's only one way to find out – ask him. Now actually asking 'what's your hand like?' is unlikely to get much of a response – unless you catch him on the hop – but by making a bet you're asking a question he has to answer. The following example shows how hard it can be to come up with an answer.

Your hand: 10s-5c
Opponent's hand: Kc-2d
The Flop: Ah-6h-2s

You've completely missed the flop but by betting you're asking your opponent – who has made bottom pair – a serious question. You're representing a hand and asking him if he believes you. If he's a tight player, he'll probably fold.

Size is everything

Before you make a bet, stop for a second to think about your objective. Do you want your opponents to call you? Or are you bluffing and want them all to fold? Keep this in mind when you make your bet, and react accordingly.

Remember that the likelihood of your being called is much higher in limit games, where your opponents can see another card for a fixed price. And keep an eye on your opponent's chip stacks. If they're heavily stacked they might call you for the hell of it, and if they're short-stacked they might be committed to calling you with almost anything.

You also have to accept that you're going to get called if you under-bet (i.e. with a small amount), and you're likely to scare someone off with an over-size bet. Bet $1 into a $50 pot

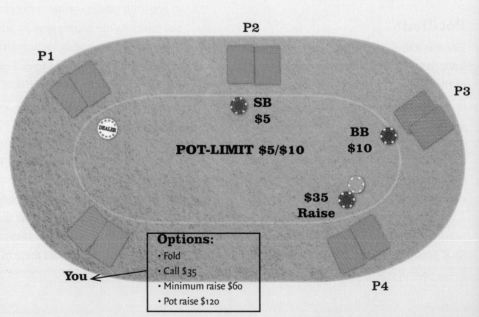

Pot-limit

In pot-limit games you can match the previous bet and then raise to a maximum of the size of the pot. In this example the pot raise would total $120 (the amount it costs to call the previous bet of $35 and then the total amount in the pot).

P1

P2

P3

DEALER

SB
$5

BB
$10

POT-LIMIT $5/$10

$35
Raise

P4

Options:
• Fold
• Call $35
• Minimum raise $60
• Pot raise $120

You ←

Asking the question

Your hand

Opponent's hand

The Flop

You missed the flop but a bet could still win you the hand

TIP

Watch players when you are out of the game, or not even playing in the game. Try to estimate their hands based solely on their betting patterns. Though you won't always see their cards in a showdown, it's a good habit and will pay great dividends.

and the chance of your opponent folding is practically zero. Make it $150 to win $50 and they're going to think twice.

Money talks

All of which is another way of saying, don't see your chip stack as winnings, see it as currency. You can use this currency to chase off chancers hoping to get lucky, to bully weak, short-stacked players or players who have tightened up because they're on the bubble (the last position before a money finish in a tournament), and you can use it to buy information.

If it costs you chips to learn that the player to your left is the sort of player who likes to check-raise every time he hits a pair on the flop, consider it chips well spent. And remember, if you don't take the initiative in betting, you'll only win when you've got the best cards. And that means you'll end up losing in the long run.

Above all else though, don't bet to patterns that your opponents will be able to read. If you only ever raise with a premium hand, your opponents will cotton on quickly and adjust their play accordingly. Be unpredictable, vary your bets, and make your opponents work for

their chips. Remember that your opponents are picking up information off you every time you bet. Make sure you feed them something that confuses the hell out of them.

Triple the blinds

How much should you bet if you've got a hand? It's very important not to over-bet as you'll drive any paying customers away. It's also important not to make it so cheap that you get a multitude of callers that heavily reduce the chances of you holding the winning hand after the flop.

Tripling or quadrupling the big blind has become the accepted norm if you've got a strong hand and want to clear out any stragglers. It's also a good way of representing a strong hand and ensuring you get called only with premium hands, a situation that you can use to your advantage later in the hand.

In the example on the next page you are the first to act and make a bet of three times the blind. All players fold bar one. It makes sense to assume that this player is holding a medium pair, or a premium hand such as A-K, A-Q, etc. You've shown strength and he's happy to call. A raise would indicate a big pair, probably Kings or Aces.

The flop provides low cards and you can safely assume that you still have the best of it, as the only cards you fear in your opponent's hand would be a Four and a Six (to complete the straight), or a pair of Threes, Fives or Sevens (that have now become

Triple the blinds

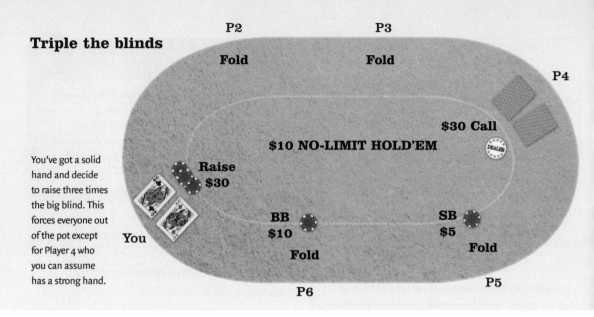

You've got a solid hand and decide to raise three times the big blind. This forces everyone out of the pot except for Player 4 who you can assume has a strong hand.

three-of-a-kind). Your opponent had to make a call of $30 to see the flop – the question you have to ask is whether you believe this player would voluntarily put that much money into the pot holding cards like that? This is where any knowledge you have gathered about your opponent comes into play. As it is, though, you'd have to assume that you still had the best of it, something that would probably be proved with another bet.

Slow-playing

In the same way that you might bet without a hand to represent strength, you can choose to slow-play a made hand to try to show your opponents that you are weak. This can have the desired effect of bleeding more chips out of them but it can also backfire if you allow your opponents to complete a drawing hand. We're not saying you shouldn't do it, but you do need to be careful. The following

Triple the blinds

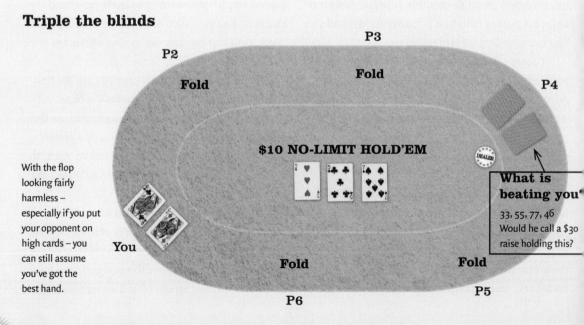

With the flop looking fairly harmless – especially if you put your opponent on high cards – you can still assume you've got the best hand.

example is a very good illustration of the inherent dangers of slow-playing a hand.

Your hand: As-Ks
Flop: Ac-Kh-4d

You've flopped a monster hand here, but you've already raised pre-flop and another big bet is likely to scare off your opponents. Slowing down could well tempt your opponents into bluffing, not to mention the likelihood of trapping anyone who is holding an Ace or King in isolation.

Your hand: As-Ks
Opponent's hand: 10s-Jh
Flop: Ac-Kh-4d
The turn: Qc

You checked on the flop to try to build the pot, but the turn has brought a Queen. Your opponent has made his straight and you're in danger of losing all your chips. This is the risk of giving players more cards when slow-playing. Would you rather be guaranteed winning a smaller pot now, or risk

WARNING!
Slow-playing is an effective way of getting more action, but it also leaves the door open for other players to turn their hand into a winning one.

being beaten to make a larger pot? The more hands you experiment with, the better you'll handle this dilemma, but keep an eye out for straight and flush possibilities before you tap the table.

Positional betting

If you're sitting in a late position, you're privy to information from everyone who has acted before you. And this means that you're in a position of strength regardless of the cards in your hand.

Your hand: 10c-4d
The flop: As-Ad-3c

If you're on the button, as you are in this hand, you're in the best position on the table and you should try to use that to your advantage. In this

Positional betting

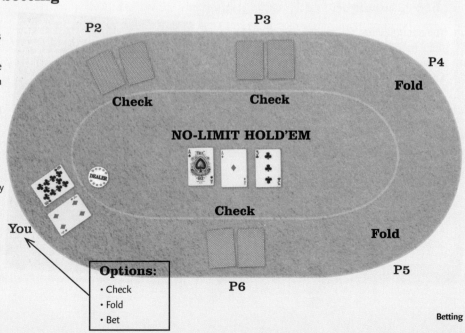

Here you're on the button, which means you've got the luxury of acting last. No one raises pre-flop, which indicates a lack of premium hands, and now everyone checks to you after the flop. Despite the fact that you haven't made a hand, and it's entirely possible that one or two of the players have you beat, any bet could potentially win you the pot.

P2 · P3 · P4 Fold

Check · Check

NO-LIMIT HOLD'EM

DEALER

Check

You · Fold

P6 · P5

Options:
· Check
· Fold
· Bet

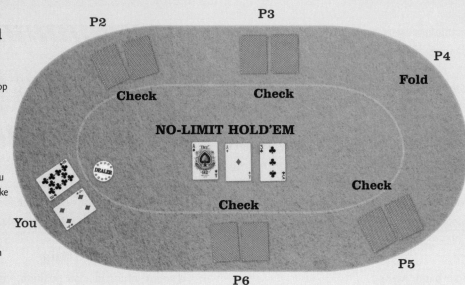

Positional betting

You might think it's risky to bet into a flop like this without an Ace but unless your opponent is slow-playing an Ace it's unlikely you'll meet any resistance. If you get raised back, make a note of the player who check-raised you, drop the hand and write it off as an investment.

example, besides having the best position you also have added impetus to act thanks to a flop packed with possibilities and the lack of action before you. This is where your observation of the table and players is paramount. If you know from experience that your opponents don't limp in if they're holding an Ace, the lack of action is an invitation to bluff with a bet. A decent bet (half the pot, perhaps) should see anyone without an Ace fold. Even if you get called (or even raised), you've effectively bought information about your opponent – and if it's simply that they are inclined to check-raise when they hit a monster hand, that's OK. The point is that your cards aren't going to win the pot, but a good bet might.

TIP

Though it's tempting, avoid using the auto-bet buttons when you're playing online. The reason for this is very simple – how can you know what you want to do until you have all the information? If you are the last to act and look down at rags (Seven and Two off-suit perhaps), don't automatically click the FOLD button – wait until the rest of the table has acted. If everyone folds round to you and you only face the blinds, a small raise might be enough to win the pot at this point. If you do meet resistance, then re-evaluate your position, but don't miss opportunities to accumulate chips. Don't write off your chances to win solely based upon your cards.

Checklist

- Betting is a powerful weapon in poker
- You can bet with a strong hand...
- And bet with a weak one...
- And both can win you the pot
- You can only win what you put in
- Betting can buy you valuable information
- Position betting is a winning strategy
- Be unpredictable
- If you're playing no-limit you can push all your chips in the middle...
- And, if you're not careful, lose them

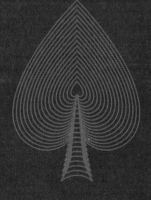

Bet like a pro and you've got a good chance of ending up with a mountain of chips

Poker Strategy

'It's hard work. Gambling. Playing poker. Don't let anyone tell you different. Think about what it's like sitting at a poker table with people whose only goal is to cut your throat, take your money, and leave you out back talking to yourself about what went wrong inside.'

STU UNGER (three-time WSOP winner)

In this chapter you'll learn...

That there's far more to poker than meets the eye. It's a simple card game, yet it's infused with a deep tapestry of subtle strategies and psychological exploration. Yes it can be hard work to start with but the rewards are immense. Your journey into advanced poker playing starts here...

There's more to poker strategy than watching *Rounders*

Poker Strategy

There are thousands of books you can buy that are dedicated purely to raising your game, but underlying them all is basic core strategy. It's all you need to play winning poker, and it's all here.

Position

We can't stress how important position is to almost every poker game. It's so important that if we were politicians we'd say this right at the start of our campaign talk, and we'd drum it in by banging our fists on the lectern and shouting 'Position, Position, Position!' So why is it so important?

Poker is all about picking up information from your opponents, gauging how strong your hand is compared to theirs, and seeing whether they're showing strength or weakness. If you're the first to act in a round of poker (known as being under the gun) you won't have any information to go on, and you'll be acting blind.

TIP

Position is vital in fixed-position games of poker like Texas Hold'em, but less important in games like Stud where the position of betting in certain rounds is dependent on the value of exposed cards.

Under the gun

In the example below you've been dealt Ks-10h under the gun. You bet three times the big blind. Player 5 folds, Player 6 calls, Player 7 raises, Player 8 reraises, Player 1 folds, Player 2 calls and Player 3 folds the big blind. You have to assume that you're

Under the gun

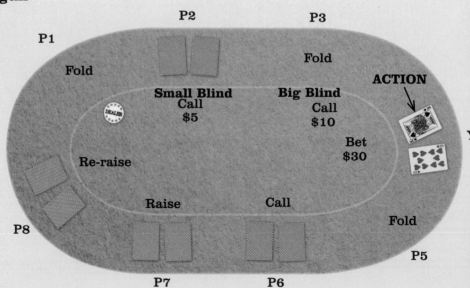

In this example you can see the problem with playing marginal hands out of position. With so many people left to act your only worthwhile option is to fold, wasting your initial bet.

now a big dog and your only sensible course of action is to fold, losing your initial bet. Don't bet marginal hands out of position.

On the button

When you're the dealer, you're the last player to act in each betting round, bar the first, where the small and big blinds act after you. This leaves you ideally placed to steal the blinds pre-flop if everyone else folds round to you. After the flop, the small and big blinds act first and second respectively, and this means that you get to see how everyone at the table plays their hand before you have to act. Position is power in poker.

In the example below you've been dealt Ks-10h on the button. Player 4 folds, Players 5 and 6 both call, Players 7 and 8 fold. You decide to raise it to three times the big blind. Players 2 (small blind) and 3 (big blind) fold. Player 4 folds, Player 5 calls and Player 6 folds, leaving you with position for the next round of betting against a single opponent. This means that even if you miss the flop, you can capitalize on any weakness from Player 5, who has to act before you. He didn't raise pre-flop so you can assume he's not

sitting on a monster. In certain situations, depending on your opponents, you can raise with any two cards in this position.

Starting hands

You should always have a strong idea of which starting hands you're going to play and which ones you're going to pass. This should always be relative to the position in which you find yourself at the table. Hands that aren't playable in an early position get stronger the closer you get to the dealer button. One of the biggest mistakes you can make in poker is to play too many hands, and it can be a hard habit to break – you play poker for fun, but you're not having fun if you're folding hand after hand.

Advanced!
Use all the basic strategies we outlined in this chapter as a guide to understanding the basics. When you've done that, feel free to move off-piste and develop your own game. Being unpredictable is good in poker.

On the button

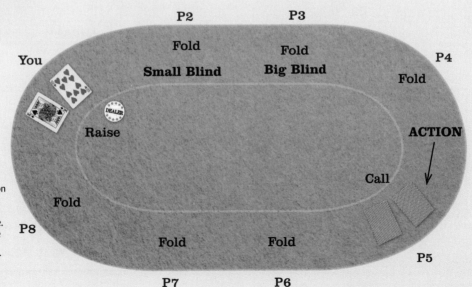

P2 P3

Fold Fold

You P4

Small Blind Big Blind Fold

Raise ACTION

Call

If you're in possession of the button you've got the strongest position on the table. Make sure you make the most of it and put pressure on your opponents.

Fold

P8

Fold Fold

P5

P7 P6

Pretty quickly, though, you'll realize that you have a lot more fun when you're winning. And to win you have to play the right hands at the right time, and learn the ancient arts of patience and discipline. We can't stress this point enough.

Table Position

In the illustration below we've split the players into three positions – early middle and late. Hands that you shouldn't consider playing in early position may well be playable as you move towards the button.

Table Position

Using Texas Hold'em as an example, the following hands could be considered playable in each position. Obviously this also depends on the action that happens at the table before you. If you're sitting in late position and the table limps or folds round to you, then you can feasibly play anything. It's also vital to remember that this is a guide from which you should develop your own plan, and that you should never play by the book. If you don't mix it up you'll be extremely easy to read.

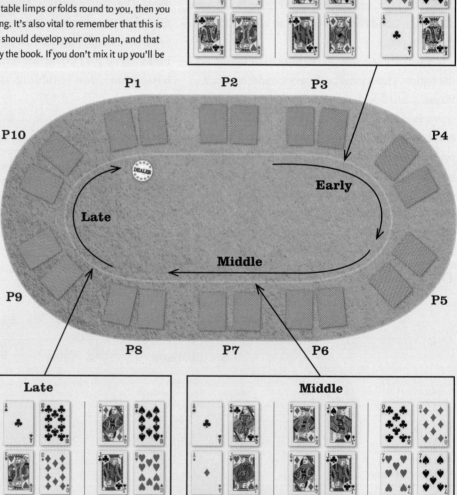

Advanced!
You might not always get a choice of seat at the table, but if you do you should quickly take stock of your opponents and try to manoeuvre yourself into the best position. As a general rule of thumb you want aggressive, unpredictable maniacs to your right (so they act before you), and passive, predictable rocks to your left. They are far more likely to let you boss them, folding their hands to any decent raise unless they're sitting on a monster. If they play back at you, you can just release your hand and try again the next round. It's amazing how often you'll get paid off.

Aggression

If position is the most important strategic consideration, aggression has to come second. Combine the two and you'll be a devastatingly effective player. Aggressive players will bet more often, play more hands and raise more often than passive players. And if you play aggressively against a rock who will only commit chips with a premium hand, you're going to get paid off regularly.

Gus Hansen is an extremely aggressive poker player, and can be almost impossible to play against

Be selective

There's no point in displaying reckless aggression. You need selective aggression – it's a winning formula. Use aggressive betting in conjunction with table position, hands, and the information you've collected on your opponents at the table. If you're on the button and the table folds round to you pre-flop, then you only have two players to get past, the small and big blinds. A raise in this position – regardless of your hand – could potentially win you the pot. The chances of the two remaining players holding a hand that they can call a raise is slim, and if they do fire back with a raise you can always drop your hand. If they call you, you might get lucky on the flop. If not, they have to act first and if they show weakness by checking (and it's extremely common for players to check back to the initial raiser), you can fire another bet at them. If they haven't connected, they'll most likely concede the hand.

Heads-up

The fewer players at the table the more aggressive you can afford to be. And when the action moves to the heads-up stage, where it's you against a single opponent, the gloves can come off. Now hands that you wouldn't normally consider playing hard become monsters. And the more pressure you exert on your opponent, the bigger the advantage you

TIP
It's extremely hard to force aggression on the poker table. If you generally play tight, try acting aggressively for a single game. Raise a lot of pots in position and see who folds and who reacts, and then try to work aggression into your general play.

have. You want to be the one constantly asking the questions, not following in his footsteps. So raise with more hands, and reraise if you think he's playing back at you with nothing. Information is absolutely vital at this stage, so it might be worth calling a few hands down – if you can justify the cost – to see how he's playing certain hands. As soon as you can gauge your opponent and start putting him on certain hands, the more likely you are to win.

Bluffing

One of the key concepts of poker is that you don't actually need the best hand to win. By betting aggressively you can knock people off a pot when they actually hold the winning hand. And, by bluffing, you can take them off a pot with any two cards so long as your timing is right and you execute the move perfectly.

What is bluffing?

Bluffing is lying about your hand, driving everyone else off the pot with a weak hand. It's what makes poker such a great game – without it you'd put money in the pot and the best hand would win. Bluffing distinguishes the good player from the bad player, and the truly great from everyone else.

Types of bluff

There are two kinds, the stone-cold bluff and the semi-bluff.

• **The stone-cold bluff:** An out-and-out bluff where you can only win the hand by forcing your opponent to fold. In the following example you've been dealt the worst possible hand in Hold'em, 7-2 off-suit, but you're feeling playful and the action has been folded around to you on the button. You put in a substantial raise but get called by the big blind.

STONE-COLD

Your hand

Opponent's hand

The Flop

You've got the worst hand, but you can still win the pot if you've got the nerve to bluff at it

Your hand: 7h-2c
Their hand: Jh-Jd
The flop: As-Ac-Qd

After the flop your opponent puts a reasonable bet into the pot. You decide that he hasn't got an Ace or a Queen and raise him a substantial amount. After thinking for a while, he's forced to muck his winning hand. Congratulations, you've just executed one of the most thrilling moves in poker.

If you're attempting a stone-cold bluff it's extremely important that you know whom you're trying to bluff. In the above example, if your opponent is a rock who plays only winning hands, the bet after the flop would indicate that he has probably connected with either the Ace or the Queen.

Similarly, if your opponent calls your raise, or even worse decides to re-raise you, it's time to admit defeat and pull out. If you've been bluffed back, then hats off to your opponent, but the chances are you're losing and in very bad shape.

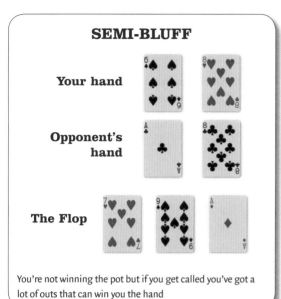

SEMI-BLUFF

Your hand

Opponent's hand

The Flop

You're not winning the pot but if you get called you've got a lot of outs that can win you the hand

• **The semi-bluff**: Here you are betting with a hand that probably is not in the lead, but it will have outs to improve and then possibly win the pot on merit if you get called.

Your hand: 6s-8h
Their hand: Ac-8c
Flop: 7h-9s-Ad

You decide to represent the Ace after the flop and bet out. Bluffing on a scare card like the Ace is very effective when your opponent doesn't hold one himself. You figure that if your opponent doesn't have the Ace he'll give the hand up, and that if he does you've still got a number of outs that could win your hand and extract a lot of chips out of him. In this instance you have run into the Ace, and your opponent decides to call your bet. The beauty of your hand is that you could still win the pot if the turn or river gives you a Five or a Ten to complete your straight. If you do hit your straight it's going to be extremely hard to spot, and you could end up winning all your opponent's chips.

Advanced!

When should you pull out of a bluff? You need to be extremely careful not to lock yourself into a bluff you feel you can't get out of. If you haven't made a hand and you fire a big bet off which is called or raised by your opponent, it's time to think very carefully about the sort of player he is and what he might be calling or raising with.

If you're convinced that he's still showing weakness then fire off another bet in the next betting round. If he's still calling or raising you it might be time to get out. There's nothing more embarrassing than being forced to show a losing bluff on the river to an opponent who called whatever bet you put in front of him.

Slow-playing

You can also make a reverse bluff, which means pretending that you've got a weak hand when you're actually sitting on a monster. This will involve a bit of acting and a strong constitution, and it can be an extremely dangerous move that can backfire if you let your opponent's draw cheaply to a better hand. Timed to perfection, though, it can leverage even more chips out of your opponents.

How often should you bluff?

There's a very easy answer to this: not very often. Bluff too much and you will get found out and, if that happens, it's imperative to tighten up. An observant table will have noticed that you're happy to throw your chips around without the best hand, and you can now use this to your advantage. Play premium hands and you should attract more action from players that have identified you as a loose cannon. After showing a few premium hands your table image will have shifted again, people will be far less likely to want to tangle with you and, picking the right moment, you can revert to the occasional bluff. Constantly mixing your game up like this means that your opponents will have

TIP

As a general rule you shouldn't try to bluff the following players:
- Maniacs – they can't help themselves and they're going to call pretty much any bluff you throw at them.
- Beginners – they don't know what they're doing so they're not going to fold their hands, even though they should.
- Short stacks – they might be forced to call because they haven't got enough chips to fold.

no idea what you're playing at any given moment, which is exactly how you want it.

Bluffing and position

We've already talked about position and how you want to be as close to the button as possible. However, if you're considering a bluff, acting first is often best.

Your hand: 10s-8h
Their hand: Jc-4h
Flop: Ac-Kd-2h

BLUFFING POSITION

Your hand		
Opponent's hand		
The Flop		

If you act first you can use it to your advantage by bluffing

Neither of you has hit the flop and it's your turn to act first. You bet out and put your opponent in an almost impossible situation. Even if he thinks you might be bluffing he can't call your bet. All he can do is reraise you (which is an incredibly dangerous move) or fold his hand. Nine times out of ten he's going to do the latter, especially if you raised pre-flop, indicating strength.

Obviously this gets more dangerous the more players are left to act. It's an exceptionally brave (or foolhardy) person who decides to bluff when there are another six players left to act. The chances of someone connecting with the hand grows with every player contesting the hand.

Black magic

You have to remember that bluffing is a fine art that will occasionally backfire. The only way to get better is to practise. Start off with the semi-bluff, and maybe throw one stone-cold bluff into the mix. Remember that you don't need every bluff to succeed to make it an extremely profitable tactic. And there's nothing more satisfying than bluffing someone off a large pot, apart from revealing your cards afterwards. And if you're a good poker player you should never, ever do that, no matter how tempting it might be. Don't be tempted to bluff too much though, you'll get caught out.

Advanced!

Bluffing is much more effective in a no-limit game where you can ask someone to put all their chips in the middle of a table. It takes a lot more guts to put everything in the middle on a stone-cold bluff, but it's a frighteningly effective way of getting someone to back off. Conversely, don't try to bluff someone out of a pot in a low-stakes limit game where it's so cheap to call that your opponent will do so nine times out of ten.

Tells

So now you know how to go about bluffing your opponents, but you can be sure that, if you're trying to bluff them, they're trying to bluff you. The question is, how are you supposed to know when an opponent's trying it on, or sitting on a monster hand that you desperately don't want to start betting against? That's where tells (interpreting someone's body language or behaviour) come in. Tells are physical actions that give out information about the sort of hand a person has. Everyone has tells – even the very best players in the world – but the aim in poker is to spot them in others and to eradicate them in yourself.

TRIVIA!

Stu Ungar was rated as the most natural card player ever. He was also frighteningly good at putting people on hands, which made it almost impossible to play against him. One example of this ability came against 1990 world champion, Mansour Matloubi. They were playing heads-up when Matloubi went all-in on the river. Ungar called him, putting Matloubi on a busted straight draw – which is exactly what he had. To make matters worse he won the hand with a Ten-high, a hand that could only beat a stone-cold bluff.

Strength is weakness

One of the most fundamental rules on tells says that when someone acts strong they're actually weak, and vice versa. If you're sitting with someone who has been acting timidly the whole game and then suddenly makes a violent, slamming motion with a pile of chips, the chances are he's trying to bluff you. And when a loud player suddenly clams up and announces a raise with a barely audible whisper, you can bet that he's sitting on a monster.

It sounds obvious but it's extremely hard to avoid this sort of behaviour in a competitive game. You get dealt a pair of Aces and your instant reaction is 'Act normal!' But the very act of saying that to yourself means that your body attempts to act normal and, as a result, you start displaying extremely abnormal behaviour. So you suddenly go quiet, or freeze and stare at a fixed, distant point. And this difference in your behaviour can deliver you on a plate to seasoned poker players.

How can you spot tells?

All you have to do is watch your opponents carefully. Some players find it almost impossible to eliminate even the most blatant tells, and if you watch the hands they're forced to reveal and how they act during the preceding betting rounds, you should be able to put together a decent profile of the way they play.

At a higher level this becomes extremely tricky, and most seasoned players have spent a lot of time eradicating all but the most subtle tells from their play. You can't do much about that, but you will find that as you become a more experienced poker player you'll gradually start picking more up from the game, and start getting hunches when someone is bluffing. This isn't a supernatural power – you're just becoming more (subconsciously) aware of each player's behaviour. Go with your hunches and see how often you are right.

Advanced!

Experienced players will try to use the most common tells and reverse them to confuse their opponents. It can be extremely hard to spot a reverse tell, but if your opponent is suddenly acting out of character you have to ask yourself 'Why?' In certain circumstances it might be worth calling down a bet to see their cards. If you can do this cheaply enough you'll know what they're up to next time they try it on.

How can you eliminate tells from your own play?

It can be very hard, especially when you're a beginner. Try taking stock of how you're acting and how you play very strong hands or bluffs, and try to act the same when you're doing both. If you're finding it hard, try to visualize a very weak hand the next time you've got a pair of Aces in your hand. See it in your mind as 7-2 off-suit and play it accordingly (obviously without folding pre-flop).

So, try and adopt a standard playing routine that you stick to, no matter what cards you get dealt. Always check your cards in the same way, and always put your chips in the middle in the same way. If you're generally chatty, stay chatty whether you get a weak hand or a monster. Don't give yourself away.

Common tells

He's bluffing

· **Weird betting movements**

Your opponent's been betting by carefully sliding his chips over the line all night, and then suddenly performs with a bit of a flourish and slams down the chips like a bear. He's feigning strength but he's actually very weak.

· **A pulse in the neck**

It's almost impossible to control, but is a sure sign that someone's more nervous than they're letting on.

Some players go to extraordinary lengths to avoid giving tells away. Top pro, Phil 'The Unabomber' Laak, wears shades and retreats into his hooded top and ties it up during particularly tense moments

· **Covering the mouth**

A very common reaction to bluffing that goes all the way back to childhood. The same goes for scratching the nose.

· **The stare-down/tense mouth**

Both of these are attempts to show strength, but they actually display weakness. Don't fall for them.

He's strong

· **Moving forward on the flop**

If an opponent connects with the flop, you'll see him moving imperceptibly towards it. It's an unconscious movement so you'll have to

Advanced!

Players also give away signs that they're on a drawing hand. If two or three cards of the same suit drop on the flop and your opponent checks his cards, you can bet he's on a draw at best. Most players remember when they're holding two cards of the same suit.

look closely to spot it, but it's very common. Conversely if he doesn't like the flop, he'll move backwards.

· **Shaking hands**

This is an extremely common tell that's almost impossible to eradicate. Hands that suddenly start shaking, especially when putting chips in the middle, are showing signs of super strength.

· **Sighing**

Any sort of negative sound – it could be a sigh or a vocal 'Uh-huh' declaration – is a sign of strength. Especially when the player follows it with a straight call.

· **Looking at his chips**

If your opponent looks at his cards and then at his chips he's probably thinking about betting, and working out how much he wants to commit. It's a sure sign of strength.

Bad beats

Get used to the phrase 'bad beat' because you're going to hear it a lot when you start playing poker. In fact, apart from boasting about winning, a poker player's favourite hobby is moaning about his latest bad beat.

So what are bad beats? Bad beats occurs when a player goes into a pot with the best hand and gets outdrawn by another player with a significantly worse hand. What defines a bad beat? No matter how hard someone tries to convince you otherwise, a bad beat only occurs when it's an unreasonable outdraw, and when all the statistics were screaming that you should have won the pot.

The hand below actually happened to one of the authors. He was heads-up when he flopped a full house. His opponent didn't realize it, but the only way he could win the hand was for two out of the three remaining Aces to drop on the Turn and the River – a 0.4 per cent shot. You can guess what happened next.

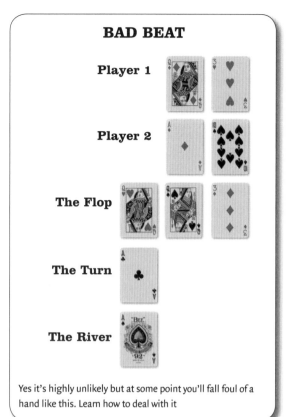

BAD BEAT

Player 1

Player 2

The Flop

The Turn

The River

Yes it's highly unlikely but at some point you'll fall foul of a hand like this. Learn how to deal with it

Player 1:	Qd-3h
Player 2:	Ad-10s
Flop:	Qh-Qs-3d
Turn:	Ac
River:	As

Now you might think that this should never happen in poker, but it will. All you can do is play good cards and hope that luck shines on

WARNING!

Bad beat stories – like the one above - are exceptionally boring. When you're telling yours, you're only marginally more interesting than an economics lecturer at 5.30pm on a Friday afternoon. Don't overdo it.

you. Remember that without the lows you can't have the highs, and just keep your fingers crossed that something like this doesn't happen to you on the final table of the World Series. Then you'd really have our sympathy. But why are we talking about bad beats in a chapter on strategy? Because if you're not careful they can lead to the poker player's worst nightmare...

Tilt!

What's worse than a bad beat in poker? Following it up by going on tilt and blowing all of your other chips. Poker's an emotional game that demands total concentration at all times, especially when you're playing in no-limit games where one mistake can cost you everything. Tilt is a condition that occurs when you have a particularly bad hand, or run of cards, whether you played them badly or you were just unfortunate enough to get horribly outdrawn.

Some people are more susceptible to tilt than others. If you're an emotional person, or someone who loses their temper easily, then you need to make an extra effort to keep things in check at the poker table. But no matter how well adjusted you are, it will happen to you, and when it does you need to minimize the damage. These four rules should see you through...

• **Treat every hand as a new hand** – no matter what happened to you the hand before, the table doesn't owe you anything. Chasing losses is the quickest way to go bust.

• **No matter how short stacked you are after your loss,** try to remember that you can still claw your way back with some careful and frugal play. Don't toss all your chips in on the next hand and admit defeat.

• **Don't play the next hand** unless it's a premium hand and then play it carefully. If you are sitting on a monster your opponents may well put you on a reckless bet, and call you. This is a double-edged sword – you want their chips but you don't want to be called by a handful of people eager to take chips off you as you might not end up favourite to win the pot.

• **Really struggling?** Take a walk. Grab some fresh air, have a drink of water, do some deep breathing and clear your head. Getting blinded off a hand or two is much better than exploding and losing all your chips.

Beware the novice

Playing against beginners isn't as easy as you might think. You've spent months studying the game and you've got its subtleties down to a fine art. Well they haven't, and they're just as likely to get lucky as you are. If you find yourself up against a complete beginner don't...

• **Bluff** He doesn't know what he's doing, so he's going to call you with just about anything. Even if there are two Aces down on the flop and he hasn't got one, he'll call you.

• **Try to read him** Again he doesn't know what he's doing or the strength of the cards he's holding, so how are you going to be able to read him?

• **Get annoyed** when he outdraws you. Poker's a game of skill and luck, and it's the luck part that keeps bad players coming back for more. You want to play against bad players, and if you play good cards you'll eventually come out on top. Don't begrudge someone their five minutes of glory when they suck out on the river. Bad beats are a part of the game, and if you want to be successful you'll have to learn how to deal with them.

Specific strategies

Here are some basic strategies to follow whether you're playing single-table tournaments, multi-table tournaments or cash games. They're extremely simplistic but they should give you a good foundation on which you can build your own game. Remember that every game of poker is going to be different, and a tactic that works on one table may backfire on another. You'll need to hone your own style and be able to adapt to different situations when necessary.

Single-table tournaments

STTs are the most popular form of poker on the Internet, and their popularity has seen them move into real-life casinos and card rooms. An STT is a freezeout tournament, where every player pays the same amount as an entry fee and receives the same amount of chips. You then play until one person has all the chips, although on a full 10-man table prizes are normally awarded to first, second and third.

The prize structure will differ from table to table, but in a full 10-man, $20 sit-and-go you can expect a payout as follows:

Total Prize Pool: $200		
1st:	50 per cent	$100
2nd:	30 per cent	$60
3rd:	20 per cent	$40

You might also have to pay an entry fee, which is the money taken by the Internet site or the casino for putting on the game. Usually this is 10 per cent of the entry fee, so you might see the sit-and-go advertised as a $20 + $2 game, where the $2 is the entry fee.

Sit-and-gos are popular because they run to a fairly standard time frame. Play a 10-man sit-and-go and you can safely reckon on being finished in around 1-2 hours, depending on whether you're playing online or in real-life (online poker is a lot faster), and with tight or aggressive players. Unlike cash games, you also know exactly how much money you're risking when you start and

how much you stand to win.

More importantly, sit-and-gos suit certain players who can regularly make some money. Something you can't say for multi-table tournaments, where you're up against hundreds of players and where you have to rely on a large slice of luck to survive.

Tactics

There are many different ways to play an STT, but no matter what your style it helps to break up the action into three distinct parts: early, middle and late. And because you know that you'll be playing against the same players until the end, it's crucial that you absorb as much information from your opponents as possible right from the off.

Early stage (8-10 players)

The blinds are going to be very low and not worth stealing. You should use the early part of a sit-and-go to watch your opponents carefully, and try to sort the maniacs from the rocks. Make a note of this and you'll be able to start stealing blinds when they're more meaningful. Also try not to get involved in any confrontations when you're not sure you're winning. Play premium hands, and be prepared to let them go if you don't connect. And only ever call an all-in if you're sitting on the nuts. (If there's a better hand, the chances are your opponent has got it. And remember, if you get to a showdown you only want to be showing premium hands.)

Middle stage (5-7 players)

By now you've weeded out a couple of the bad/unlucky players, and you should have a good idea of how the rest of the table is playing. You should also have cultivated an image that you're an extremely tight player who only plays premium hands. If this is working for you, and you've been getting good cards, you should be sitting on a

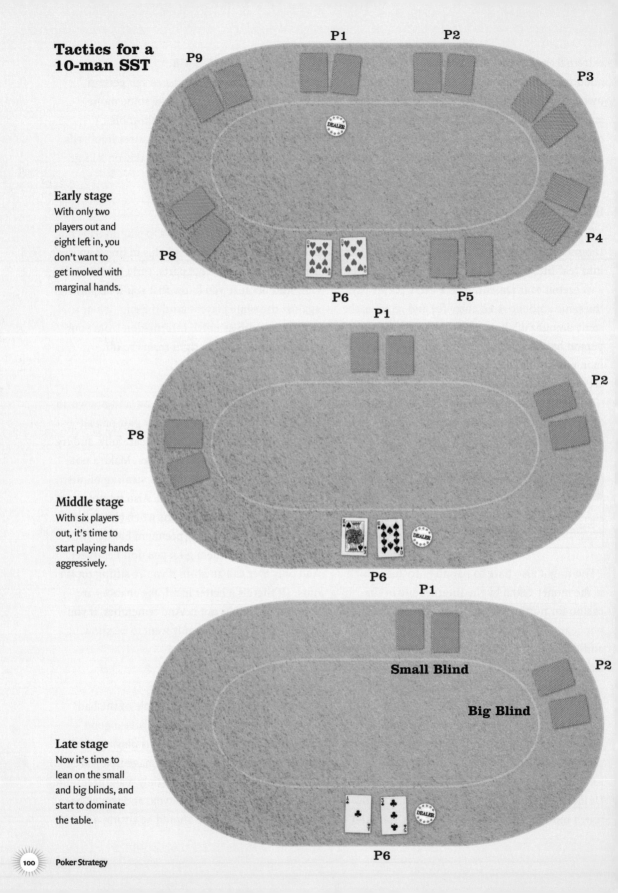

Tactics for a 10-man SST

P9 **P1** **P2** **P3**

DEALER

Early stage
With only two players out and eight left in, you don't want to get involved with marginal hands.

P8 **P6** **P5** **P4**

P1

P2

P8

Middle stage
With six players out, it's time to start playing hands aggressively.

DEALER

P6

P1

Small Blind

P2

Big Blind

Late stage
Now it's time to lean on the small and big blinds, and start to dominate the table.

DEALER

P6

fairly decent chip stack , and there's no need for you to change your tactics. If you're below the average chip stack it's time to start displaying more aggression. You can use your tight image to steal blinds (which are going to be more meaningful now) and actively target the players you've identified as weak.

Late stage (2-4 players)

You're extremely close to the money and, at this point, weaker players will start to tighten up in fear of going out on the bubble. You should be in it to win, so start playing hands aggressively that you would have folded in either of the previous stages.

Lean on the small and big blinds whenever you're on the button, and target any players who seem loath to play hands – it's amazing what they'll put down in order to make the prize-winning positions. But do beware the short stack players at this point. If they get to the stage where they're moving dangerously low compared to the level of blind in play, they might be forced to move all-in with medium hands, and the last thing you want to do is double them up.

Advanced!

You'll find that sit-and-gos differ massively depending on who you've got at your table, and you might well find that the simple strategy we've outlined doesn't work in all instances. What it does outline, though, is one of the principal strategies of successful poker playing, called shifting through the gears. As you move through a sit-and-go you should be prepared to get more and more aggressive as fewer players are left in. If you tighten up when you start approaching the bubble point, you're going to find it hard to accumulate enough chips to challenge for the number one spot – and that generally pays as much as second and third combined.

WARNING!

Six- and even five-man tables are extremely popular as you can easily fit one into a lunch break at work. And these are often played as turbo or even extreme-turbo games where the blinds go up extremely quickly to force a result in as little as 15 minutes.

Far be it from us to suggest you avoid these games entirely because they can be a lot of fun and, if you're pressed for time, they might be your only option. But one thing that they all have in common is that a lot of the skill of poker is sucked out and replaced by luck, and to that extent a lot of players consider them crapshoots. However, other players swear by them as they suit their naturally aggressive style. If you get involved, open out your starting hand selection as far as possible. The blinds are going to move so quickly that, if you sit back and wait for premium hands, the chances are you're going to get blinded out before one hits.

Multi-table tournaments (MTTs)

Are you reading this book to make a million? Well, multi-table tournaments are the best way to do it. They are the big ones, and the bigger the multi-table tournament, the bigger your prize will be. But you need a strong strategy to triumph and a big dollop of luck. You can't control the latter but, if you go in with a solid plan and stick to it, you'll deserve your luck when you get it.

First you need to decide what starting hands you're going to play and what you're going to pass. And it's no good sitting and playing tight the whole time if you're aiming to win because, by the time you get a hand, your more aggressive opponents are going to be sitting on the monster stacks they've accumulated by picking on weak players early on. From the off you need to try and split your table into two player types, the rocks who'll fold to any raise unless they've got a

The multi-table tournament is where you're going to make the big life-changing sums of money

Above all, though, remember that if you don't go all-in you can't go out. Top players try to put all their chips on the line as little as possible. Even if you go into the pot as favourite there's every chance that you're going to get outdrawn, so why risk everything? Remember that even Aces get beaten approximately one in four times. If you're lucky enough to get them four times in the course of a tournament and you're all-in every time, statistics say you'll lose once, and if all your chips are in the middle, that's your tournament over.

Cash games

Cash or ring games are different again and require a completely different strategy. In fact tournaments and cash games are so different that a lot of players play only one or the other, but not both. In a cash game the chips you're playing with have an exact monetary value and every hand you play is for cash. There's no set start and no set end – you play for as long as you want, or for as long as your money lasts.

What's your game?

It's crucial to stick to what you know best in cash games. If you're a decent Hold'em player then a move to Omaha could spell big trouble. And you need to know that high-only games are very different to high-low games. Different limits have a massive impact on the game too. The safer games are obviously the low fixed-limit games where betting is capped at a certain point (normally after three raises in any particular round), and each bet can't go above the stated limit.

No-limit games are extremely risky in a cash game. If you've entered a game with your entire bankroll then you could find yourself going bankrupt in one hand. Be extremely careful, and try not to go into a game with any more than you can afford to lose.

premium hand, and the other aggressive players, like you, who want to boss proceedings. You don't want to get drawn into a life-threatening pot early on, so it's important to avoid people like this. Be selective about when to be aggressive. Use your position wisely, and be prepared to back off if one of the tight players suddenly plays back at you, unless you're sitting on a monster.

As you move through the tournament keep an eye on your chip stack, both in relation to the average and the other players on your table. Try to keep yours above the average at all times and, if you start getting short-stacked, make a move before you get to a position where you don't have enough chips to scare others off the pot. In fact, the bigger your stack the more aggressive you can be, and the more creative you can be when you're selecting starting hands, but don't get carried away. Getting too aggressive and getting involved in pots you shouldn't be in, or calling with weaker hands just because you can afford it – that's the quickest way to turn your big stack into a short stack.

Advanced!

You might think that the worst place to finish in a poker tournament is last, but you'd be wrong. It's much, much worse to battle through a huge field, playing poker for sometimes days on end, only to get knocked out in the very last position before the money. This is known as going out on the bubble and it can be heart breaking.

So, what better way to accumulate chips than to attack medium stacks when the bubble's approaching? We say medium stacks because it can be dangerous to attack a short stack when your opponent might be forced to move all-in. Players with medium stacks know that if they sit tight they're likely to make the money, and that if they don't get involved unnecessarily they might make the final table where the prize money goes up steeply. Take advantage of them, but again use your prior knowledge to avoid aggressive players who still have their eye on the first prize – they'll probably bite back.

Tips for cash games

It's extremely important to gauge your opponents as quickly as possible. Do they consistently draw to hands they're unlikely to make? Are they loose and aggressive? Or are they only betting when they've got made hands?

The quicker that you can pigeon-hole your opponents, the quicker you'll be able to modify your game accordingly. And the nature of cash

TIP

Limit games are less prone to wild bluffing. When it only costs one more bet to see your opponent's cards, a lot more hands go all the way to the showdown, and this means that you generally need a bigger hand at the end to take it down. Don't keep betting on hands that you think are losing.

games means that you're likely to be sitting with the same people for a long time.

Cold run

If you're not getting cards then just get up and walk away (or click the sit-out button if you're playing online). Take a break, get some fresh air and clear your head. If you really feel that it's not your night, pack up your chips and leave. There's no point in chasing losses in a cash game when things aren't going right – you'll invariably make things much worse.

Stick to your plan

If your plan was to spend $50 and leave if you go bust, stick to it. It's always tempting to buy back into a game, especially if you've been busted out on a bad beat. Try and resist – it's the quick route to poverty.

Play a cash game and all the chips that you're betting with represent real sums of money

Advanced!

You might find yourself mastering a certain limit game, and if you're winning consistently you should consider moving up a level. It might take a while to find your feet in the new game but it will be worth it financially. And don't be tempted to skip one – the gulf in class will be too big, and you might move out of what's termed your comfort zone and start betting amounts you can't afford to lose. When that happens you'll invariably play losing poker.

Advanced!

You might think that it makes sense to take as much money as possible to the table to put you up with the chip leaders but, in a pot or no-limit game, this could be a mistake. If you enter the game with a small buy-in, you can call an all-in without fear of losing your entire bankroll. And this could actually stop you getting bullied off a big pot when you don't want to commit all your money.

Outs.	2 cards to come	1 card to come
1	4 per cent	2.2 per cent
2	8 per cent	4.3 per cent
3	12 per cent	6.5 per cent
4	16 per cent	8.7 per cent
5	20 per cent	10.9 per cent
6	24 per cent	13.0 per cent
7	28 per cent	15.2 per cent
8	32 per cent	17.4 per cent
9	35 per cent	19.6 per cent
10	38 per cent	21.7 per cent
11	42 per cent	23.9 per cent
12	45 per cent	26.1 per cent
13	48 per cent	28.3 per cent
14	51 per cent	30.4 per cent
15	54 per cent	32.6 per cent
16	57 per cent	34.8 per cent

50x the big blind

Not sure what level of cash game you should be playing? $1- or $2-limit games might sound cheap, but pots get big very quickly. The general rule is that you should go into a game with no less than 30x the upper limit. That means that to play comfortably in a $1-2 limit game, you'd need $60. Go in with less than this and you'll be severely hampered and unable to sustain any sort of bad run with the cards.

Pot odds

We talked about basic pot odds in our Hold'em chapter, and if you're playing cash games it's essential that you know the basic maths behind the game. Stripped to its most basic level, it's a game where you're putting money in (i.e. your bet) to take money out of the pot. It's obvious that if you're a favourite to win the hand you should always bet. But how do you know if you're a favourite? And what if you're behind? Should you call another bet in the hope of your hand improving, or should you cut your losses and get out? You need to know if you're getting favourable pot odds.

You can use this table to calculate your chances of winning a hand, or use the following simple formula. It's not scientifically accurate but it's close enough...
• With two cards to go, multiply your number of outs by four.
• With one card to go, multiply your number of outs by two and then add two.

Now consider the following example.

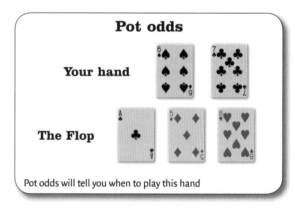

Pot odds

Your hand

The Flop

Pot odds will tell you when to play this hand

Your hand: 6s-7c
The flop: Ac-5d-8h

Example one – good pot odds
The pot: $150
Your bet to call: $15

In this hand you've flopped an open-ended straight draw, but you're convinced your opponent has the Ace and he has just fired another bet into the pot. You have eight outs (four Fours and four Nines). With two cards left (the turn and the river) you have a 32 per cent chance of making your hand. As you're only being asked to put $15 into the pot, you're getting favourable odds for your money (you're getting 10/1 for a 4/1 bet).

Example two – bad pot odds
The pot: $100
Your bet to call: $50

Here you've got the same number of outs and the same shot at making your hand – 32 per cent – but, in this instance, you're only getting 2/1 on your money with a 4/1 chance of making it. You should fold the hand.

Advanced!

When should you leave a cash game? It's undoubtedly true that you should leave if you're running cold in a game and you've lost your initial buy-in. Chasing losses never does any good. But there are some who say that you should have a fixed idea of an amount that, once hit, should also signal the end of the game. The thinking behind this is that as a cash game has no fixed end, if you carry on playing endlessly you stand a good chance of losing everything you've won. And there is some truth in this. Carry on playing for days on end and you'll be fatigued, and you'll start making some very bad decisions. But say you find yourself in the best possible game. You're with chumps who insist on betting every pot, even though they've got nothing in their hands. All you have to do is bet with good hands and you can't lose. Should you leave this game? Hell no. Stay for as long as you can and take all their money. Dream tables like this don't come around very often, so make sure you make the most of them. Do try and keep a record of your wins and loses though. It's the only way of knowing whether you're winning or losing.

Checklist

- **Position is power**
- **Selective aggression is a winning tactic**
- **Good starting hands are the foundation of solid poker**
- **Bluffing is a powerful weapon**
- **Everyone has tells – it's just a case of looking for them**
- **Everyone suffers bad beats**
- **But not everyone goes on tilt afterwards**

chapter 7

Online Poker

'It used to be that if you didn't know who was at your table, you were at a good table. Now you find yourself sitting next to a guy who seems like a random Swede, and he turns out to be a million-dollar-winner on the net.'
DANIEL NEGREANU (Professional Poker Player)

In this chapter you'll learn...

The Internet has helped poker hit the mainstream, so look out for a raft of new big-budget films this year, including *Lucky You*

That you don't have to leave your house to get a good game of poker. Virtual card rooms are up and running 24 hours a day, 365 days a year, and they're packed with people like you playing cards for cold, hard cash. What's more you can learn the game by playing for free, before moving up and playing for millions in your own bedroom. What are you waiting for?

Online Poker

Play poker whenever you want, for however long you want, without leaving your home. The beauty of the Internet is that in cyberspace there's always someone wanting to play you at cards.

Millions of people are playing poker on the Internet every day, and the numbers are growing all the time. It's revolutionized the game and brought a new breed of player to the table because, while you're playing to the same rules, the nature of online poker makes for a markedly different experience.

For a start, you don't have to handle cards. Shuffling, dealing and looking at your cards are all taken care of automatically. You can't act out of turn, you can't make illegal bets and you don't have to worry about your personal hygiene. All you have to do is decide what sort of game you want to play, how much you want to spend and whether you want to check, bet, raise or fold by clicking on the relevant button. And this has a dramatic impact on the game.

The differences

You'll immediately notice that poker on the Internet is...

· Faster

Internet poker is much, much faster than real-life poker. If you're playing a standard online game you get about 30 seconds to make a decision before you're timed out and checked/folded automatically. However, decisions are often made instantly – sometimes by using the auto-bet buttons – and it means you'll be

Decide how much you want to bet and click the button – that's all you have to worry about when you're playing poker online

In a standard online game you get approximately 30 seconds to make your decision. Fail to act in time and your hand will be checked or folded automatically

seeing up to 60 hands an hour, approximately one per minute. Play in the real world, where you have to shuffle, cut, deal and physically move and stack your chips, and you won't play anywhere near this number, even if you've got a professional dealer.

· **Looser**

Because online poker is faster, and you get less time to make your decisions, it's looser. Add to the equation the fact that a lot of people play multiple tables simultaneously, or play while watching TV, and you can get an *extremely* loose game with people playing hands they wouldn't touch if they were in a casino. This is helped by the fact that you don't have to put up with people laughing at you from across the table when you have to show the 7-2 off-suit you've been playing aggressively on a flop of Aces and Kings.

There are pros and cons. The good news is that a loose game is rarely boring. There's plenty of action and plenty of dead money to take. On the other hand you're going to have to put up with more bad-beats and accept that you're going to

get called – and possibly beaten – by any number of weird starting hands.

· **More accessible**

Games are available whenever you want them, and you can play for as little or as long as you want, which sounds brilliant. And it is, if you play responsibly. But get on a losing streak and it's all too easy to chase cards and end up losing even more money. If you feel you're hitting a cold run of cards online, then get out for a day or two before going back. Don't make the mistake of playing bad poker just because it's there.

· **What sort of games can you play?**

As in the real world, Texas Hold'em rules the online roost – over 80 per cent of online poker at the last count – but if you're a fan of Seven-card Stud and Omaha, you can find a game on all the big online sites. More specialist games like Five-card Draw and Triple Draw are available, but you need to hunt around to find them.

The main choice is between play and real money tables, and between cash (or ring) games and tournaments. Online cash games are the same as you'll find in the real world, with varying limits from $0.25/$0.50 games up to dizzying $500/$1,000 games where thousands of dollars can be won or lost in a single hand.

Freerolls

Freerolls tournaments are free to enter but provide real prizes. And if they sound good, they are. There's no real problem apart from the fact that they're immensely popular, and are usually packed with hundreds and sometimes thousands of players all clamouring for the same prizes.

Generally, the bigger the prize, the more people you'll get playing. The Paradise Poker Million Dollar Freeroll is the ultimate example. As the name suggests, it's a free-to-enter tournament that provides an amazing $1 million first prize. The downside? You'll have to battle past thousands of players to qualify for the final. And then past thousands more to get to the final table (usually played live in an exotic location).

The catch? There isn't one. You're not paying any money, and even if you don't win you'll get

TIP

You could spend your whole life searching for freerolls on the Internet. Time that would, quite frankly, be better spent playing poker. Which is where the fantastically useful www. freeroll-tracker.com comes into its own. It doesn't list tournaments from every poker client, but it lets you browse through a myriad of different free-to-enter tournaments and saves you a lot of time. Make sure there aren't any entry conditions (like loyalty points), and that the prize is worth investing time in. Battling through thousands of people and spending upwards of five to six hours for a prize of $10 is only for the foolhardy.

invaluable tournament experience. However, the nature of the freeroll means that the play is even looser than the loose Internet play. Which means it's *incredibly* loose – especially in the first hour of the tournament when some players decide the best strategy is to double through quickly and often. Try to avoid any confrontations early on, unless you're in possession of the nuts.

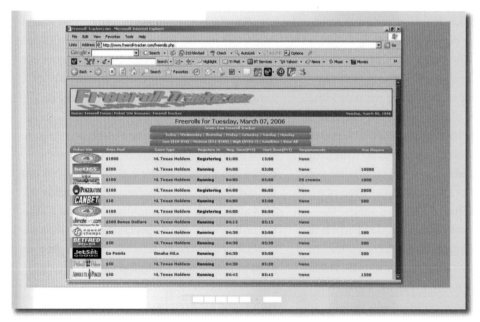

Find the best freerolls at www.freeroll-tracker.com

Can't afford the buy-in for the Ladbroke's Poker Million tournament? Qualify through online satellites for as little as $10 every day

Satellite qualifiers

Fancy entering the World Series of Poker Main Event, but can't stump up the $10,000 entry fee? That's where satellites come in. Satellites are qualifiers to bigger tournaments – either online or real-life – and let you play in big money games for a small initial outlay.

Proof that this stystem works is the story of Chris Moneymaker, who entered a World Series satellite for $30, won a ticket to the Main Event, ended up winning the whole tournament and pocketed a cool $2.5 million. Not a bad return on his cash.

Online you can find satellite qualifiers to every major tournament, and some unique packages such as poker cruises and TV tournaments.

Internet strategy

Remember that online poker plays to the same rules as offline poker, so you can use all the general poker strategies we've given you so far. There are also some online-specific tips you need to conquer the online game.

· **Playing for free**

Join any online site and you'll be given a certain amount of play money, which you can use before you make a real money deposit. Now it's true that poker is a gambling game, and without the risk of money you lose a large part of the game. So why would you want to play for free on the Internet? There's a simple answer... To get better without getting poorer.

There's a myth surrounding free money tables on the Internet – that nobody takes them seriously and that you can't get a decent game. But that's not true. Free money tables are packed with people just like you, who are using the gift horse to get better before risking real money. Sure, you'll find a few maniacs who call anything and everything just because they can, but they're few and far between.

Also remember that playing for free is a winning strategy. It doesn't matter who you are, when you start playing poker you'll be losing much more than you'll be winning, but the amount of time you keep on losing depends

You can use the free tables to practise games or formats you're unfamiliar with before risking your own money

how quickly you learn. For some people it's a month. Others need a few months to hone and perfect their skills. But whatever the length of time, it's immensely profitable to spend it on the play tables. Build up your skills and confidence here, and then think about making your first real money deposit.

· **Money management**

When you start playing for money you'll find that it's extremely easy to lose track of how much you're spending. Make sure you keep an accurate record of how much you've deposited, how much is still in your account, and ultimately whether you're up or down on the whole deal.

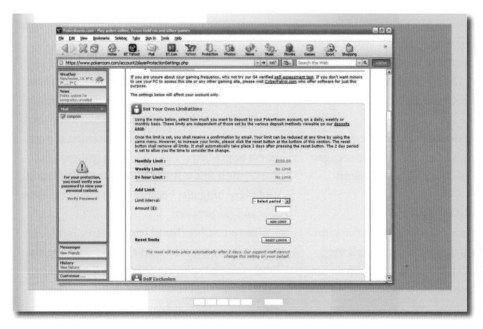

Play responsibly at all times – decide how much you can afford to lose and set your own limits

Use www.recpoker.com for tips from around the world

Decide what you want to get out of the experience. If you're playing poker to make money then you shouldn't have to keep making deposits. This is a sure sign that you're losing. If you're just playing for entertainment and you don't expect to make a profit, decide how much you can afford to lose per month and don't put any more money in your account. You can set your own levels on most online sites – this is the amount per month that you don't want to exceed. Hit this amount and it won't matter how hard you try, the online site won't take your cash.

The bottom line is that if you're playing for real money you should play responsibly at all times. No one's going to stop you from gambling away all your hard-earned cash if you're not prepared to stop yourself.

· Distractions

Distractions are the scourge of the online poker player. If you're playing in a casino, the only thing to do is study your cards and opponents. Play in your living room and the distractions are almost endless – you could feasibly be playing

TIP

The Internet is awash with poker sites and forums offering help and advice on anything with which you might be struggling. The best starting point is rec.gambling.poker, a newsgroup that lets you post messages and share information with other poker players across the world. You can access it through your regular newsgroup application or browse through the web-based newsreader at www.recpoker.com.

If you're playing poker on the Internet, turn the TV off and concentrate on the cards

poker while watching TV, surfing the Internet, cooking dinner and talking to your partner. And it might seem obvious, but these other activities will have a massively detrimental effect on the quality of your poker.

Everyone knows this and yet almost everyone does it. Don't fall into the same trap. If you're playing poker, concentrate. If you want to watch the big game on TV and eat a toasted cheese sandwich, turn your PC off.

· Multiple tables

Unless you've got a doppelganger, you'll only be able to play one game of poker at a time in the real world. This isn't true on the Internet, where you can play many tables simultaneously. In fact a lot of professional players swear by playing more than one table at once on the basis that if they're winning consistently on one table, they'll win four times as much by playing four tables.

Now this may be true for some, but not everyone. Some people find it physically impossible to deal with more than one table, while others claim that it's not possible to play

optimum poker unless you're focusing on one game. Our view is that online poker is fast enough without having to spice things up, but you should do what feels right for you. If you find that your brain can cope with numerous decisions, and you're playing winning poker across a number of simultaneous games, then go for your life. If it feels wrong, and you're getting stressed at having to make snap decisions then just play the one table. As with anything to do with poker it's about what works best for you. However one thing you definitely shouldn't do is play more than one table until you're an extremely experienced player.

Advanced
You can take advantage of people who are trying to play more than one game at once. Browse through the tables and look for recurring names. When you find a player who is playing a few games simultaneously, put yourself into one of the games. Then observe the other games they're playing and if you see them getting involved in a big confrontation, you can bet you're not going to meet much resistance from them.

You can play multiple tables online if your brain can handle the action, but you need to be extra sharp to deal with the rapid decisions that are going to be thrown your way

· Online tells

Every time you're dealt a big pair you start shaking and sweat profusely. It's a bit of a giveaway in real life, where players can see you across the table. But it's not a problem online where your opponents can't see you, your hands or your perspiration. However, this also means you can't rely on getting visual clues from your opponents, something that's a huge part of the game in real life.

That's not to say that you can't pick up other signals online; you just need to be looking for different things. And in the absence of physical traits, your opponent's betting patterns are the best way to decide what kind of player they are, and whether they've got a strong hand or are trying to make a move on you.

Look for the amount of time they take to make a decision, and when they deviate from the norm. And look at the sort of hands they're raising or limping with pre-flop, and try to guess what cards they've got in their hand in the future. It's amazing how often you'll get it right. See if the player on the button keeps attacking your big

blind. If he's raising you more than 50 per cent of the time, then you can be sure that he's not waiting for premium hands. Use this information and – unless you get unlucky and your timing's wrong – he'll probably back off.

Also try to identify the tight players who always fold unless they connect on the flop, and the aggressive players who always bet on the flop regardless of their cards. And keep an extra-sharp eye out for anyone you suspect is using the

TIP

The speed of Internet poker means you're going to see more hands and should be able to spot betting patterns a lot quicker – as long as you're vigilant. If you're watching TV or paying your household bills while your opponents are betting, you're going to be playing blind. And try to avoid falling into predictable patterns yourself. Take the same amount of time to make every decision, tough or straightforward. Don't give yourself away by sitting frozen, staring at the pair of Aces you've just been dealt before putting in a huge raise.

Watch out for players using the auto-bet buttons and don't be tempted to use them yourself

auto-bet buttons – there's no easier way to follow someone's betting patterns. And don't use them yourself. They might be tempting, but bar typing your hole cards into the chat box it's the best way of letting your opponents know exactly what you've got in your hand. Make your opponents work for information – never give it away for free.

· Make notes

How are you going to keep all this information in your head? Easy – make notes. Play online on the same site regularly and you'll see the same names cropping up time after time. You can give yourself a massive advantage in these games by making notes on these players for when you next play them. A lot of online sites actually provide a note-making facility on the interface, so you can just click on the relevant player and type in a few lines. Next time you're playing against them you'll be able to access your notes instantly and play accordingly.

Say you're playing against Player X and you notice that he only ever raises pre-flop if he's holding an Ace or a big pair. If he's holding an Ace and connects on the flop he'll carry on playing aggressively regardless of his kicker. If he doesn't – and he's not packing a big pair – he'll generally fold to any meaningful bet. He's playing very basic poker and being able to recall that information with the click of your mouse means you'll be able to pick him off at will, and avoid losing much when he's packing a real hand. When you've developed a list of bad players, look for them every time you're online. A lot of sites let you search for players by name. If not, scroll through the tables manually.

And while you're actively targeting people, make sure you keep an eye out for:

· Players on tilt

Look for people losing a really bad hand and then betting big the very next time they get dealt cards, and players expressing their anger in the chat box. If they're bothered enough to type ANGRY things, you can bet they're really RAGING. And if they're RAGING they're ripe for the taking. Don't waste time replying if they insult you. Play carefully and hit them hard when

Make notes on the good or bad players you encounter, and you'll be at an advantage next time you play them

TRIVIA!

We've told you not to get drawn into conversations when you're playing online poker, and it's good advice. But if Jackie Johnson and Gary Suffir had listened they wouldn't have found true love. They met playing in a $30 Omaha game on Party Poker in September 2004, six months later were living together and they got hitched in March 2006. Apparently they're now trying to start a family, and they're going to call the baby Chip if it's a boy. Strange but true.

you get good cards – ignoring them and then taking even more of their chips is guaranteed to wind them up big time.

· People who love to talk

Some people spend more time typing into the chat boxes than they do playing their cards. Try it for yourself – if you're feverishly typing great witticisms into the box it takes time and, before you know it, the action is round to you again and you're forced into making a snap decision. Watch out for the talkers and lean on them. And try not to get drawn into lengthy conversations yourself. You're not there to make friends.

· Maniacs

Maniacs love throwing their chips around for the sheer hell of it, and you'll find more playing poker on the Internet than anywhere else. Join a sit-and-go online and more often than not you'll see someone moving all-in pre-flop, with only the blinds to pick up. It's a terrible play – if the maniac's got a strong hand then he's not going to get any action. If he's got a middle-to-weak hand he's risking everything for the sake of a few chips. Don't get drawn into any unnecessary confrontations, but when you get a monster, hit him hard. Make sure that you're the one he gives his chips to.

Am I going to get ripped off?

We've established that online poker is brilliant. You can play it whenever you want, at whatever level, in the comfort of your home. You can even play it in your pants, and according to official statistics about 10 per cent of people do. But one question remains…

Is online poker safe?

It's reasonable to assume that if you're going to give your credit card details to someone on the Internet you want to know they're on the up. And we're going to do our best to convince you that – so long as you stick to the list of reputable sites at the end of this chapter – your money is safe. Despite extremely vocal claims in online forums, online poker isn't rigged. Play good poker and you'll win. Play bad poker and you'll end up losing money. And it's the bad poker players – funnily enough – who are the most vocal critics of online sites.

The facts

Poker is an established business. All reputable sites use the very latest encryption software to keep all your credit card details safe. You have to provide the number, the name on the card, your address and the security number (the three digits on the back of your card) before you can put any money in your account. And putting money into an online poker account is as safe as buying from any of the massive Etailers, like Amazon.

Why online sites won't cheat

The big online poker sites have been going for years and make a huge amount of money by taking a cut from all cash games and charging for tournaments. If you see an online tournament advertised as a $10 + $1 game, the $1 is the fee charged by the online operator.

Online operators take a rake from every cash hand that's played

In the example above, a cash game is in progress at the popular online site PokerRoom. The hand number – 199, 345, 758 – is displayed in the top left corner. The pot is currently $93 and the rake – the money taken by PokerRoom from this hand – is $2. Multiply the number of hands by the rake and you can see how much money online operators can make legitimately.

Party Gaming, the company that owns PartyPoker, one of the world's biggest poker sites, recently floated on the London Stock Exchange and the initial valuation put it *ahead* of British Airways. It makes almost $1 million a day in profit, and it does this by keeping players and providing a secure environment for playing poker. If the software was rigged, or if sites like PartyPoker or PokerRoom were cheating people out of their money, they wouldn't go back. Why would companies like this risk these ridiculously huge – and some might say vulgar – profits by rigging games?

Why online sites can't cheat

The backbone of any poker site is the software,

and this is provided by a number of separate companies like Boss, Excapsa and Cryptologic. All of these use RNGs (random number generators) to try to ensure that all the cards are dealt in a random fashion, and that each shuffle at the start of every hand is as thorough as is scientifically possible. (And a perfect shuffle isn't something you're going to see at your local casino, in fact only a handful of people in the world can claim to have perfected it.) Independent auditing checks that this happens in every poker hand that's played on the Internet.

What happens if I lose my connection?

It's extremely rare if you're with a reputable service provider but, if you are unfortunate enough to lose your connection mid-game, most online sites give you about 30 seconds to reconnect. So, if your PC shuts down for no reason, or your connection fails, just reconnect to the Internet, fire up your poker software and you should be automatically taken back into your game. However, if your downtime is considerable and you're playing in a cash game, you'll be taken out of the game temporarily (and you'll be considered all-in for any chips you were betting in that current hand). Your seat will be held for a few minutes, but if you don't reconnect you'll be taken off the table.

If you're playing in a tournament, you'll still be dealt cards and you'll still have to post blinds, but if there's a bet against you, your cards will be folded. If the blinds are high you won't last long, but if it's in the early stages of a tournament it'll take a long time for you to be completely blinded away. Funnily enough, it is possible to make it into the money if your connection's down and you've got enough chips to make it past the bubble.

What about the other players?

We're not saying that cheating doesn't happen. It does, but it's extremely rare and the sites are doing everything possible to ensure that it's stamped out almost immediately. Report any suspicious behaviour; just click on the Help or Contact button and you'll immediately be able to fire off a message to the operator. In particular, look out for...

· Collusion

It's a form of cheating – as old as the game itself – where two or more players co-operate to give themselves an advantage over other players. In live games, players collude through coded signals and gestures. You might also collude by dumping chips on to a colleague to strengthen his stack, putting him at an advantage in a big-money tournament. It's something that's impossible to completely eradicate from the game, but vigilance can keep it to a minimum.

In an online game, where no one can see what you're doing, it's a lot easier to collude. Unscrupulous players can easily communicate their cards with other players on the phone, or through a chat application like MSN. They might even be sitting in the same room and playing on a network. But while it's easier to collude online, the nature of online poker means that it's much easier to catch and deal with anyone doing it. Online sites have access to every hand ever played, and they employ dedicated staff and use the very latest software to monitor and track suspicious patterns. If collusion is proven, accounts can be suspended, money frozen and even refunded to players who have been cheated out of their cash. Again, report any suspicious behaviour to the operator.

· Bots

The beauty of poker is that it's a matching of minds, a game of skill between humans, not a game like Blackjack that pits you against the house advantage. But can you be sure that you're playing against real people? Poker bots are computer programs that play for you, using artificial intelligence to make decisions. In theory, this means that they can play a solid game, without deviating from solid poker strategy, for 24 hours a day. They'll never draw against the odds, and they'll never get tired or click the wrong button by mistake.

Terrifying? Not really. The current levels of artificial intelligence just aren't good enough to cope with the complexities of poker, especially the more human elements such as bluffing. Online poker sites still take poker bots seriously, though, and actively track anyone attempting to use a bot, and they'll freeze accounts of anyone found to be using one.

TRIVIA!

At the 2005 WSOP, top pro Phil 'The Unabomber' Laak challenged the winner of the World Poker Robot Championship – PokerProBot - to a game of heads-up Texas Hold'em. He considered himself a favourite going in and identified weaknesses in the bot's strategy. And yes, he won.

Which site should I play on?

There are so many online poker sites vying for your business that most of them try to tempt you with a unique promotion or the promise of something for nothing. Shop around before you sign-up, and take advantage of the latest offers.

Sign-up bonuses

Sign-up bonuses are extremely common and are normally promises to match your first real money deposit up to a certain limit. So, if you sign-up and deposit $100, the online site will promise you a $100 bonus. There is a catch though – you normally won't be able to access this bonus money until you've played a certain number of pay tournaments or raked hands on the cash tables. But bonuses aren't to be sniffed at. At the end of the day it's free money for playing poker, and it can often arrive in your account at the most opportune time.

Loyalty points

In the same way that supermarkets try to keep you coming back for more with a loyalty card, online poker sites try to keep you playing at their tables with regular player point schemes. And in among the bog-standard giveaways like T shirts and baseball caps, you can find some useful schemes that offer you tickets to 'exclusive' freerolls and satellite qualifiers. Whatever you do though, don't get dazzled by offers that seem too good to be true – they invariably are!

We unearthed some pretty earth-shattering giveaways researching this book, including a site that was offering a brand new Mini-Cooper in return for 60,000,000 (yes, 60 million) player points. Playing at the rate we do (and we play a lot), we worked out we'd need to play for a mind-numbing 26 years to earn enough points to bag one. By which time you'll be zipping around in a hover-car.

All you need to play poker online

Top 10 poker sites

All of the following online poker sites come highly recommended (and no, we're not on a commission, unfortunately), and offer something unique, from exclusive satellites to big-name pro players. Stick to the sites on this list, and you'll know that you're playing in a safe and secure environment.

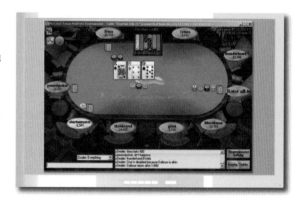

Paradise Poker
www.paradisepoker.com

Home of the Million Dollar Freeroll, which lets you play for the chance to win a million dollars for free. The first ever million-dollar winner was Lee Bidulph, a 28-year-old chef from Blackpool. He got flown to the sun and beat nine other Internet qualifiers on the live final table. Play your cards right and you could be next, although you'll have to beat thousands of other hopefuls.

PokerRoom

www.pokerroom.com

Poker can be a lonely business. It's normally you against the world in a game where collusion and teamwork is frowned upon... Unless you're playing in PokerRoom's unique Team Tournaments where you can hook up with your mates and gang up on the opposition. It's a lot of fun.

PartyPoker

www.partypoker.com

One of the biggest and most established online poker sites in the world, and home of the PartyPoker.com Million Cruise, a huge limit Hold'em tournament that takes place on a cruise ship in the Caribbean. Lots of people means plenty of fish to take money off.

Betfair Poker

www.betfairpoker.com

Betfair made its name in the sports betting world, when it took out the bookie and let you bet directly with other users. It's also an extremely popular online poker site that's developed an excellent reputation with its regular users. You can find a wide variety of games and a pretty good standard of play, and qualify for a major tournament with Betfair and you'll get treated like royalty.

Poker Stars

www.pokerstars.com

The self-styled 'home of the world champions', Poker Stars is the site to play on if you want to qualify for the WSOP. Poker Stars takes more players to the World Series than any other online site and for a few dollars, you can win worldwide fame and a fortune. Chris Moneymaker, Greg Raymer and Joe Hachem – the last three winners of the WSOP – all play on Poker Stars.

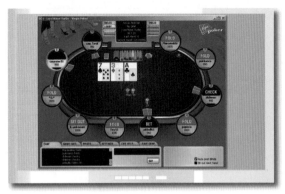

Virgin Poker

www.virginpoker.com

One of the newest additions to the burgeoning online poker scene, Virgin Poker is the place to play if you want to turn your loyalty points into something other than baseball caps. Using Richard Branson's connections you can swap them for flights on Virgin Atlantic and other Virgin commodities. And if you're concerned about the reputability of online sites, surely you can trust the cards dealt by Richard Branson.

Ultimate Poker

www.ultimatepoker.com

Home to some of the world's best players, Ultimate Poker stages the Aruba Classic, an annual tournament that a lot of pros cite as their favourite of the year. It's in the Caribbean, which means that if you qualify you either win lots of money or get to kick back on the beach, a true win/win situation. And if you want to qualify online, you have to do it here.

Full Tilt Poker

www.fulltilt poker.com

Want to mix it with the pros? Full Tilt is the place to play with some of the biggest and best players in the world affiliated to the site. Phil Ivey? Chris Ferguson? Mike Matusow? The Hendon Mob? Erm... Check, check, check and check, and if you're lucky you can find them online and challenge them to a game.

Ladbrokes

www.ladbrokespoker.com

The traditional UK bookmaker is now one of the biggest forces in UK poker. Its Poker Million tournament is now the biggest Hold'em tournament outside the US – the recent 2006 Poker Million V final boasted a whopping $4.2 million prize pool. You can qualify for as little as $10 through daily satellite tournaments.

PKR

www.pkr.com

Launched by a group of talented video game developers, PKR is a sophisticated 3D site that aims to bring some of the tells of real poker into the online game. It looks amazing and doesn't lose anything in the translation from 2D. Not for the Old School, but definitely the funkiest site for playing poker on. Expect to find a load of younger players playing here. And enjoying themselves.

Checklist

- You can play online poker 24/7, 365 days a year
- Texas Hold'em is the most popular online game
- But you can find Omaha, Stud and Draw as well
- It's generally fast and loose
- And you can play for free and win real money prizes
- Online satellites let you qualify for huge tournaments for a few dollars
- Online sites don't use rigged software
- And though cheating's possible
- It's extremely rare and easy to trace

Poker's not the only game you can play online – Blackjack's becoming very popular as well

chapter 8

Home Games

'Marriages may come and go,
but the game must go on.'
FELIX UNGER (The Odd Couple)

Jack Lemmon
(foreground)
knew he would
lose his head in
a chaotic home
poker game with
Walter Matthau
and friends in the
hilarious 1968
comedy The Odd
Couple

In this chapter you'll learn...

How to host the perfect home game. We'll show you how
to avoid the most common pitfalls, and give you the
rules you need for a night of harmonic bliss. You just
concentrate on cleaning up the money and the mess.

Home Games

Playing in multi-million-dollar tournaments is all well and good but nothing can beat a good home game with your mates – as long as it's run properly. We're here to make sure that your game is the best home game in the world.

As poker becomes increasingly mainstream, and people take it more seriously, it's important to remember that poker's supposed to be fun. Which is where the home game comes in. It's still important to have rules, but everything you need to know, you can find here. However, before you start worrying about the details you need to decide whether you want your home game to follow a cash game or tournament structure.

Cash game

In a cash game each player buys chips at their actual monetary value. So, if you put in £20 you'll get 20 chips worth £1 (or whatever denomination you choose to play with). Every hand is then played for money. Once the game is deemed over, or players decide to leave, they can cash in their chips according to their value.

Tournament

Playing to a tournament structure has many advantages. There's a set start and finish which means the game won't go on indefinitely, it limits the amount of money that you can lose in one night and, more importantly, there's an ultimate winner who gets to gloat and become the enemy for the next game. In

You can buy simple poker table-tops from most high-street stores

a tournament structure, each player buys-in for the same specified amount and everyone gets a specified number of chips. There are two main types…

· Freezeout

The freezout is simpler to run. Everyone buys in for the same amount, everyone gets the same amount of chips at the start and, when they're out, they're out. With no second chance, you tend to get a tighter game with everyone protecting their chips far more than in a…

· Rebuy

Rebuy tournaments let you buy back in to the game when you've busted out. To stop the game going on for ever, rebuys are limited either by time (e.g. you can make an unlimited number of rebuys in the first 60 or 90 minutes) or number. When you rebuy you normally get the same amount of chips with which everyone started, but you're usually given high-denomination chips (other players can change them for smaller denominations). This stops the table getting flooded with small change. Normally, after the rebuy period is over, everyone then gets a chance to add-on. This means that regardless of how many chips you have, you can put the rebuy amount forward and top up your chip stack with the additional chips a rebuy would have given you. Because of these extra 'lives', rebuy tournaments are usually much more aggressive than a freezeout. They tend to go on longer (because of the extra chips on the table) and the prize pool is much bigger.

The kit

You don't need much to host the perfect home game – a pack of cards, some chips and a dealer button (or pepper pot if you're desperate). But if you're planning on your game becoming a regular fixture, you should seriously think about getting decent kit. It doesn't cost that much to buy quality gear, but it makes a huge difference.

Advanced!

Another popular type of tournament is the Double Chance. As well as getting your starting chips, you can buy a second lot at any point within a set time limit. You can take them at the start to give you more chip power early on, or wait and take them if you bust. Aggressive players tend to take them at the start so they can bully. More cautious players prefer to use them as an extra life, effectively giving them two all-in opportunities.

Make sure you buy a decent set of chips

Cards

They have to put up with a serious amount of fingering and shuffling, and cheap paper cards won't last. They bend easily, and bent cards make it harder to deal effectively, and they're harder to conceal from your opponents. Look for a pack of 100 per cent plastic cards because they're much more durable and won't mark. These cards might be a more expensive initial investment (although you can pick up a half-decent set these days for a couple of quid), but they'll last much longer and as well as working out cheaper in the long run they're much nicer to play with.

Chips

You can't play without chips. Playing for cash is no good – you won't have the correct denominations – and matchsticks are far too fiddly. Decent, relatively inexpensive sets are readily available. A couple of years ago you'd only find poker chips in specialist shops or on the Internet. Now almost every decent high-street store stocks a selection. Don't be tempted to save a bit of cash by going for the cheapest and nastiest kind; they're an affront to the poker gods. Try to find a set that is made of clay or clay composite. They're heavier (normally 11.5g) and much more satisfying to push around and riffle with. Most sets come with a plastic dealer button; if not, buy one. It's better than using a coffee cup.

How many?

The amount of chips you need for a game depends on how popular you are. If you've got a full complement of 10 people, you're going to need a full set of 500 chips. If you decide to play a tournament structure, it's extremely important to start everyone off with the right amount of chips.

Make sure you buy enough chips for the number of players you're expecting at your game

TIP

If you're playing with chips that don't have denominations marked on them, try to stick to a single system. This avoids confusion, incorrect bets and stops you having to remind everyone how much their chips are worth every five minutes. You could try making the chips increase in value the darker in colour they get. So, yellow = $25, red = $100, blue = $500 and black = $1,000. This also makes it much easier to see how much your opponents have got in front of them.

Too few and it'll be a lottery before the first level; too many and you'll still be there 24 hours later. Though you can buy chips with the denominations shown, the majority of sets are blank, allowing you to use them as you choose.

Blinds

The blinds are easily the most important part of a home game. The blinds dictate the pace of the game, how aggressively players will need to play to survive, and how long the game will last (depending upon your starting stack). This is achieved through increasing the blind levels at regular intervals throughout the game.

Besides controlling the progression levels (for example, doubling every level or following another fixed pattern), you can also decide how often the blinds step up. If you increase your blinds every 10 minutes, you'll get a fast, turbo-charged game without the luxury of sitting back and waiting for premium hands. Stick to more traditional 30-minute levels and you'll get a lot more play. This might suit beginners who need longer to settle into the game, but be warned – if someone goes out early they're going to have a long wait to get back in the game.

The only way to find the right structure is to experiment. If you find that something's not working, just tweak it the next time you play.

Here are a few tournament suggestions to get you started:

Starting stack: $2,000

Small blind	Big blind	Level duration
25	50	20 mins
50	100	20 mins
100	200	20 mins
200	400	20 mins
400	800	20 mins
500	1,000	20 mins
800	1,600	20 mins
1,000	2,000	20 mins

With 20-minute levels there's plenty of time to play before the blinds become steep and put pressure on you.

Starting stack: $2,000

Small blind	Big blind	Level duration
25	50	15 mins
50	100	15 mins
100	200	15 mins
150	300	15 mins
250	500	15 mins
350	700	15 mins
500	1,000	15 mins
1,000	2,000	15 mins

An entirely different style of game, with faster blinds and a different sort of blind structure. Rather than stepping up in a logical style, these blinds are designed to push the action along, as – after the first hour – the increments become far steeper.

Prize pool

You can distribute the prize pool however you want, but it's important to establish the winnings before the game begins. If there are only four of you, with a £5 buy-in, you wouldn't want to pay any more than first and second, or possibly winner takes all. If there are seven players, a first and second prize make sense, and possibly even a third. If you pay down to third the following structure is the best: first place gets 50 per cent of the prize pool, second place gets 30 per cent and third place 20 per cent. Then again, you could change the balance so that first gets 60 per cent and third gets 10 per cent. You decide.

Tables

Once you've played hours of poker hunched over a coffee table, you'll realize how important it is to play on a proper surface and with decent seats. You can buy a specialist table or a cheaper table-top, but it's a lot easier to make the best of what you've already got. Remember:

Don't

- Play on a glass table – the cards will slide everywhere.
- Play on a dirty table – the cards will pick up dirt and deteriorate.
- Play on a shiny surface – people might be able to see cards as they are dealt.

Do

- Have all players sitting at the same level so no one can accidentally (or deliberately) see the cards as they are dealt or held.
- Invest in a few metres of felt or artificial baize to cover the table-top – it'll make all the difference.
- Include breaks in any long games so players can stretch their legs.
- Provide ashtrays and drink mats to preserve the playing area.

Housekeeping

Avoid any possible arguments (always likely when money is involved) by clarifying the rules before you start. How strict are you going to be? Will you ignore string bets? Will you give people a hard time if they talk about their hands? And will people be punished if they keep bidding out of turn? These points might seem trivial, but once the game

TIP

As you get towards the end of your tournament you should colour up the chips. This means swapping the smaller denominations for larger ones (only if you have spare chips to bring in). The $25 chips that were valid in the early stages will become annoying by the time the blinds are $600 and $1,200. The standard practice is to round-up any odd chips, so someone with $125 in $25 chips should get $200 in $100 chips.

has begun it's very hard – and hugely unpopular – to introduce rules as you go along, especially if you're drinking alcohol. Many a home game has broken up in drunken squabbling because the rules weren't made clear at the start.

The buy-in

Think about the people playing before you decide upon the buy-in. If your primary objective is to make money, then you want as much money in the prize pool as possible. If, however, the game is primarily a social event, then the buy-in needs to be an amount that won't hurt people if they lose. If anyone loses more money than they think they can afford, they won't come back next time. And a successful home game is one where everyone returns with a smile. Having a decent prize pool is a great way to make everyone take the game seriously, but if the game ends with good friends sulking off into the night you've clearly got the amount wrong.

The gene pool

If it's a social game, don't invite people who won't get on, and don't invite players who might go soft on each other. Disaster!

Errors

Here are two common mistakes to avoid, or problem areas that often need resolving in home poker.

• **Acting out of turn** This is more a symptom of Internet players who've never had the option of acting out of turn before, and they end up throwing their cards into the muck with three players still to act, or raise out of turn, ruining the game. Make it the dealer's responsibility to clarify whose turn it is to act, and remind players of their options. If a player continues to act out of turn, you could impose a light punishment like a short suspension. If you do impose rules like this, make sure everyone knows what they are at the start.

• **Splashing the pot** (or throwing your chips into the main pot). When each player bets, they need to keep their chips separate from the pot so that the amount can be checked quickly and easily. If space is limited, make it the dealer's responsibility to direct players to keep their bets away from the main pile and gather the pot.

Blinds in empty seats

When a player gets knocked out, it can affect the blinds. If a player who was about to be the small blind leaves, the blinds can't just move round as the next player in sequence will have missed the big blind. The simplest way to tackle this problem is to place the dealer button as if the player were still there. So if the departing player was due to be the small blind, then there is no small blind in that round – only a big blind. If the departing player was due to be the dealer, you should place the button in his empty space (he's then known as a dead dealer) so that the proceeding players don't miss a round of full blinds.

If the departing player was due to be the big blind, then the sequence continues and the player to the left of the departed player becomes the big blind one hand earlier than he would have done. Basically, no one should ever be at an advantage or disadvantage when a player leaves the table.

WARNING!

By all means drink but getting bat-eyed means players will misdeal, expose cards, act out of turn, talk about their hands and generally be extremely annoying. Don't be a spoilsport but do try to keep control of the game. It's you they'll all blame if things go wrong.

Misdeals

There are a variety of mistakes that can be made during the deal. Here are some of the commonest...

- If any cards are accidentally exposed during the initial deal, all cards must be retrieved and the hand is declared a misdeal. Shuffle and deal again.
- In flop games like Texas Hold'em, if the flop is delivered before the betting round has been completed, the exposed flop is taken back and discarded. A new flop must be dealt once the initial betting round has been completed.
- If a burn card is accidentally exposed, all players must be made aware of the card before it is then turned face-down, and play continues.
- If a player exposes any of his cards when throwing them into the muck, all players must be made aware of the exposed cards, and play continues. If a player continually does this, give a warning.

TIP

It's unlikely that anyone will attempt to cheat in such a cosy atmosphere, but one rule that will keep everything above board is to stipulate that cards and chips must be kept on the table at all times. You might also want to check that no one attending has the same chips as you, and has sneaked a couple of extra $1,000s into the game!

Checklist

- Buy a decent poker set – cards and chips are a must
- As is a decent surface and seating
- Decide on the format – cash or tournament
- Set the blind structure to suit the length of the game required
- Don't make the buy-in so big your friends hate you when they lose
- Make all the rules clear to everyone before you start
- Drink, but not too much
- Make sure everyone you've invited gets on
- But not so well they go soft on each other

Live Games

'Whether he likes it or not, a man's character is stripped bare at the poker table; if the other poker players read him better than he does, he has only himself to blame. Unless he is both able and prepared to see himself as others do, flaws and all, he will be a loser in poker, as in life.'

ANTHONY HOLDEN, author of *The Big Deal*

In this chapter you'll learn...

That taking your online poker skills to a casino or card room is about more than simple geography. Etiquette, presentation, conduct and possessing a reasonable poker face become far more important. A lot of people forgo the experience because they think they'll be exposed as novices and picked on. We're here to make sure that that doesn't happen.

Robert De Niro in the Scorsese classic, *Casino*

Live Games

Perfect your poker face, pack your sunglasses and make sure you've got Kenny Rogers's *The Gambler* on your iPod. It's time to take your new-found skills out into the real world.

A lot of today's seasoned poker players (unlike those of the past) have never set foot in a card room. The accessibility of Internet poker and the comfort of playing in your own home has meant that a lot of players have never fingered a chip, despite having played a hundred thousand hands in their time. They're missing out. Live poker is a completely different and massively rewarding experience. A fantastic social game, live poker also offers the opportunity to find out just how good your poker face is or if, indeed, you have the ability to read tells in others.

There's nothing quite like playing live poker, and it doesn't have to be an intimidating experience if you know what you're doing

Casino and card room memberships

Recent changes to gambling laws have made it far easier for you to make spontaneous visits to the casinos and card rooms in the UK. Previously you'd need to join and then wait for 24 hours before you could play in a casino. Now, so long as you've got a passport or a driver's licence, you can walk into a casino any time you want and start playing within minutes.

Many casinos and card rooms have websites listing live tournaments, as well as details regarding cash games. One slightly old-fashioned ruling you might still encounter, though, is a dress code. If you're a tourist in Las Vegas then all but the most elite poker rooms will allow any dress (within reason), but many of the capital city casinos of Europe still insist on smart attire, including jackets for the men.

In the card room

Once you're in a card room, the first thing is to find out exactly what games are being played. As poker becomes increasingly popular, the quality of these rooms is always improving, but you should expect anything from the highly detailed plasma screens of Las Vegas poker rooms to felt pen scribblings on a white board in East London. The poker room manager, however, remains the key to everything. Besides being able to tell you what games are currently running, he can also tell you how many players are waiting while being able to sign you up for forthcoming tournaments.

Due to their popularity online, more and more live rooms are now running what are called sit-and-go tournaments, where a mini-tournament begins as soon as enough players are available. If you are mostly a tournament player but don't know tournament schedules in advance, keep your eyes peeled for these quick-fix opportunities.

Live games

If there's one game you can almost guarantee finding in a live room it's Texas Hold'em, but in a large card room you can also find Seven-card Stud and Omaha. Certain card rooms also like to run a dealer's choice table, where a vast variety of strange and varied poker variants are played. Be very careful about sitting down at one of these unless you know your poker games inside out. Limit, no-limit and pot-limit are all normally catered for, but don't be tempted if it's not a limit or structure with which you are familiar.

Self-dealing

Unless you're in a big-money tournament you may well be expected to shuffle and deal until the final table. If you're more at home clicking a mouse than dazzling opponents with your shuffling skills, this can be a daunting prospect and might spoil your experience. There are various flashy ways to shuffle, but if you watch professional dealers you'll see that the best way is to spread the cards out across the tables and give them a super-random swirl. Take time to practise before going public.

In most live games a simple sequence is used to ensure safe, random shuffling. The player to the left of the dealer shuffles the deck, the player to the right of the dealer then cuts the pack, and then the deal begins. It's also your responsibility to ensure that the deal is clean and fair, so be sure to keep the base of the deck concealed, and don't rush the deal because it can lead to accidental exposure of cards.

TIP

If in doubt, copy how the other players shuffle and deal. The last thing you want to do is give anyone the impression that you are any less experienced than they are!

The comfort zone

Besides knowing how to deal, there are a number of unique elements to live games that can easily catch you out. You need to be at ease with everything in a live game so that you concentrate fully on your cards. One of the easiest ways to achieve this is by allowing yourself time, on your first visit, to watch the proceedings. Watch players handling the chips, the sequence of play, tipping of the waitresses, racking chips, posting blinds, you name it. You don't want to sit at a table and look silly, so be sure you know how everything works before joining in.

Chips

Chips are your new, best friends, so be nice to them. If you don't treat them well, they'll leave you. When you're at a table, stack your chips sensibly. Random towers reaching into the sky are begging for a fall, and won't make life easy when you need to reach for a specific amount. By stacking your chips in a way that makes sense, you should always be able to see how many you have at a glance.

And when making a bet, don't dramatically hurl your chips on to the table. You might have seen it done in the movies, but it's this kind of splashing the pot that gets you on to players' hate lists. Move your chips around like a pro, and make sure you announce what you're doing. You get much more respect if you act and bet in a controlled fashion.

WARNING!

If you are asked to move tables (for instance when tables break down during a large tournament) you *must never* put chips into your pocket. Anyone seen putting chips into their pockets or bags risks losing their chips and being ejected from the tournament. In any live game there should always be chip racks available but, if there aren't any, ask the dealer or room manager.

2004 World Series of Poker champion, Greg 'Fossilman' Raymer with one of his now famous card protectors

The buy-in

In most of the larger poker rooms you'll have the option of either buying chips at a main desk, or simply sitting at the table and requesting chips *in situ*. Just put your money on the table and the dealer will call for chips. You can also get more chips this way if you run low. When it's time to cash-out, take your chips back to the main desk and they'll turn them back into (hopefully) wads of cash.

The colour-up

If you play in a large tournament that has break periods, don't be concerned if you return from a break to find that some of your chips appear to be missing. To make chip management easier during the latter stages of a tournament, the chips are coloured-up. This means that lower denominations that were useful in the early stages are now defunct (what use are $25 chips when the blinds are $2,000 and $4,000?). The good news is that you will find that the amounts are usually rounded up so, for instance, if you had $150 in $25 chips, you'll receive two £100 chips in return.

Cards

Whether you are acting as the dealer or just one of the players at your table, it's your responsibility to look after your cards. When dealing, take care to shuffle them well, avoid damaging them, and make a clean deal. Missing out players on a busy table, or dealing in such a way that everyone is scratching their heads wondering which cards are theirs is not how to make friends and influence people. Also...

- When players fold their cards, you must retrieve them and keep the table as clear as possible.
- When you're playing, be sure to protect your cards when you look at them, when you place them in front of you.

TIP

Many players like to put a chip from their stack on top of their cards to indicate that they are still 'live'. Many players also have lucky charms or custom card protectors.

WARNING!

Don't be tempted to show any friends or new pals at the table any of your hidden cards when folding. Many tables have a show one, show all rule, so you'll end up having to show your cards to all the players at the table. And that's way too much good information for free!

- If you plan to fold, try not to handle the cards in a way that makes this obvious (i.e. holding them like a Frisbee, ready to fly across the table when it's your turn).
- When you plan to continue playing, protect your cards so that the dealer doesn't mistake them for dead cards and gather them into the muck.

Table talk

Depending upon where you go to play, the amount of table talk you encounter will vary wildly. Some tables seem to encourage plenty of friendly banter, while others are filled with iPod-listening, sunglass-wearing silent strangers. Wherever you find yourself, there are a few rules you should always follow...

- Never discuss your hand, regardless of whether it's still in play or mucked, until that hand has completely ended.
- Never react in a way that affords any live players information about the hand you've just thrown away. So, if you just dumped 2-6 in a Hold'em game and the flop comes down 2-2-2, don't start slapping your head and swearing.
- In fact, don't ever swear.
- Never insult other players or the dealer.

Waitresses

If you're lucky enough to play in a card room with waitress service, you can ask for drinks and food without having to leave the table. Depending on the location, you might even find that drinks are complimentary. It is, however, customary to tip the waitress, especially in the States. If you are in a cash table, you can chose to tip using either cash or chips with a cash value. You cannot, of course, tip using tournament chips that have no direct cash value.

Dealers

Many players like to tip dealers after winning a pot in a cash game, especially in the USA where dealers are notoriously underpaid and rely on tips to supplement their income. The size of the tip is entirely down to your discretion, but is generally dictated by the size of the pot. In a low-limit cash game, just a dollar chip is sufficient. If the pot is worth much more, the size of the tip should increase proportionately.

Leaving the table

In a cash game you are totally within your rights to leave the table for extended periods of time. If you need to stretch your legs, grab some lunch or visit the toilet, you only need to let the dealer know and he will look after your chips. He will post your blinds and fold your hands as they orbit the table. It's not good etiquette to leave for hours at a time, though, because there might be other players waiting for your seat, and the other players are going to want a full table. But don't think that you're obliged to sit there until you leave the game.

TIP

If you're nervous about how much to tip, watch a game before entering and note how much the current players tend to tip depending upon the size of the pot. Then all you have to worry about is winning a pot to tip from!

Advanced!

Just because you have your headphones on doesn't mean you're listening to music, does it? Players who don't think you're listening often get slack and betray slight tells. Put them to the test.

Table toys

Apart from custom card protectors, players bring all kinds of strange things to the table. Expect to see a variety of lucky trinkets and toys sitting by some players, and a wide range of hats, dark glasses and music systems. Wearing sunglasses to mask any visible tells is perfectly acceptable, as is listening to music. Generally, you will be asked to keep your music to a level where other players can't hear it. You might also be cautioned if you are repeatedly slow to act or misunderstanding plays because you can't hear audible instructions. Most tables are very tolerant of any strange behaviour provided it doesn't interrupt play or annoy other players.

Wait your turn

This is the most common mistake made in a live game. The easiest way to avoid it is not to look at your cards until it's your turn to act. This way, as well as being absolutely sure it's your turn to act, you'll avoid giving any tells until you have to. If you're dealt pocket Aces and have to wait 30 seconds before reaching for your chips, you'll probably be shaking like a leaf by the time the action is on you.

TIP

When you find yourself up against a player in a heads-up situation over a big pot, once it has concluded, pull out your note pad and appear to make reams of notes. No poker player likes to think that they have any tells, so making lengthy notes can unsettle their play.

Take notes

Online players don't think twice about making notes about their opponents, so why should it be any different in a live game? Don't be afraid to carry a book with you to make notes about plays (your own as well as your opponents').

Tells

Being invincible on the tables while sitting behind a PC screen is one thing. Reproducing a winning performance in front of a room full of opponents – all keen to relieve you of your money – is another thing. You'll have more to think about, and the fact that your opponents can see you means that it's important not to give any tells away about the strength of your hand. This isn't as easy as it sounds. Quite often you're going to be completely unaware that you're doing something, until it's pointed out by someone else; it might be as innocuous as scratching your nose every time you're bluffing.

One thing is certain, though – you will have tells. So before you start looking for tells in others, check yourself for habitual behaviour in certain situations. Probably the most basic tell is showing strength when weak, and vice versa. Try to police yourself, and be sure your actions are consistent, regardless of the situation. If you place chips into a bet when strong, and then throw chips at the table when weak, someone will spot this.

Also try to moderate how long you take to make a decision. Even if you look down at junk, count to five before mucking the hand. If you then count to five when calling or raising, no one can associate your timing with the strength of your hand. And if you talk at the table, be careful not to give information away with idle chat. Maybe even decide that you never talk when involved in a hand. If someone asks you a question and you ignore them, simply wait until the hand is over and then tell them that you never talk during a live hand.

If you watch the big-name poker pros on TV you'll see they generally fall into talkers and non-talkers. When a talker manages to get a non-talker to reply during a big hand, you can be sure that some tiny piece of information will have been picked up during the exchange. Don't be lured into talking, unless you believe yourself such a great actor that you can fool an opponent.

And as previously suggested, play with friends and family and ask them outright if you exhibit any tells. If they tell you that your eyes tend to dart around when on a big hand, wear sunglasses. If you look at your watch when drawing, take it off! One of the simplest ways to eradicate tells from your game is first to look at your cards only when it's your turn to act, and second to turn to stone as soon as you make any moves. Stare at a spot on the table and don't move until the hand is completed. See the Strategy chapter for more advanced information on tells.

Ask for help

Don't be afraid to ask for help. If you're unsure of a situation, or have a query, just ask the dealer. If you have a larger issue – for instance a complaint about another player – then call over the floor manager to resolve any problems. Never sit in silence if you are unhappy about a situation. And if you disagree with the way a dealer managed a hand, or think someone is trying to bamboozle you, call for help. It's your right as a player to feel 100 per cent comfortable in any situation.

Finding games

As poker becomes more popular, finding live games becomes easier. There is now a vast online community of poker enthusiasts all running non-profit groups dedicated to nothing more than getting together and playing poker. Generally you can find simple set-ups with small groups playing single-table tournaments, as well as low-limit cash games. Surf the net and see what you can find.

Checklist

- Live poker is a brilliant and social experience
- You can now walk into a casino or card room and play instantly
- Watch a game in progress before taking the plunge
- Make sure you can shuffle, deal and handle chips properly
- Etiquette and courtesy will win you as many friends as pots
- Police your behaviour and eradicate as many tells as possible
- Talk as little or as much as you like at the table, but always be polite
- Take as many toys to the table as you want, but always consider your fellow players
- Look beyond the obvious places to find good live games
- If in doubt, ask

Video Poker

1

'You cannot survive without that intangible quality we call heart.'
Bobby Baldwin (Professional Poker Player)

In this chapter you'll learn...

That video poker isn't like normal poker. For a start you're playing against the house, which means that unless you go in with a solid strategy, you're bound to lose. However, as a fun diversion from the serious card rooms of the Las Vegas casinos, video poker is well worth playing. And if it's worth playing, it's worth playing properly.

In Las Vegas you can watch the Bellagio fountains going off. Or you could go and play video poker and get a free drink

Video Poker

You might have seen the rows of people sitting at the casino bar, feeding dollars into bar-top machines, taking advantage of the free drinks and occasionally whooping with delight. This is what they're playing...

Video poker first appeared in the 1970s, and has remained one of the most popular forms of gambling in the USA ever since. There are a variety of different types, with the possibility of hitting some large jackpots.

Although video poker is an extremely simple game there is an element of strategy that can lead to a much higher return than on pure luck games, such as slots or roulette. One of the biggest attractions is the low house edge it operates under, coupled with the element of fun (it's basically a cross between poker and a slot machine). Play it optimally and it's possible to find some machines with a return of 99.5 per cent, and that's about as good as it ever gets in a casino!

It might not be an equal playing field but you can still have a lot of fun taking on the casino

Pay to play

If you're new to video poker, you won't want to risk too much money learning the game. There is a wide range of games on offer, with credits set at anything from 5c right up to $5 a go. Find a machine where you can wager more than one credit per hand without spending more than you can afford. The majority of machines you will encounter in any American casino will be 25c, 50c and $1 machines.

The rules

Video poker really couldn't be any simpler. You decide how many credits you want to play with, from one to five, and you're then dealt five cards. You can choose to hold any or all of these cards before the machine takes your discards and deals replacements. If you've completed a five-card poker hand that is recognized by the pay-out schedule of the game you are playing, you are paid off for any wins. The wins vary depending upon the game being played, but will typically begin at even money for a single pair and move up from there.

Payouts and game types

The most important consideration, when selecting a machine to play on, is the payout table. Even the slightest tweaking of these payout structures by the casinos can make an enormous difference to your expected profits. Compare machine with machine, and game with game.

Jacks or Better

The following table shows a sample payout schedule for a Jacks or Better machine. To qualify for an even-money payment, you must at least make a pair of Jacks. This payout also assumes that you are playing five credits a turn to maximize any payout. The PAYS number refers to the number of credits returned (e.g. here you

are betting five credits to play, and Jacks or Better gives an even return).

Hand	Pays	Frequency
Royal flush	4,000	1 in 40,390
Straight flush	250	1 in 9,148
Four-of-a-kind	125	1 in 423
Full house	45	1 in 86
Flush	30	1 in 90
Straight	20	1 in 89
Three-of-a-kind	15	1 in 13
Two pair	10	1 in 7
Jacks or Better	5	1 in 4

The table below shows a machine that rewards four-of-a-kind hands highly. As you can see, depending upon the rank that builds your four-of-a-kind, the payout varies wildly. In this instance, hitting a four-of-a-kind can actually be far more profitable than making a straight flush. A royal flush pays out a specific cash amount rather than a controlled return.

Hand	Pays
Straight flush	250
Four-of-a-kind aces	800
Four-of-a-kind 2s, 3s, 4s	400
Four-of-a-kind 5s thru kings	250
Full house	45
Flush	30
Straight	20
Three-of-a-kind	15
Two pair	5
Jacks or Better	5

Very nice. If you've been playing the maximum credits you've struck gold

In this final example you can see the impact wild cards have on the schedule. Because of the improved odds with four wild cards in the deck, the lowest hand that's paid out is three-of-a-kind, which only receives an even payment. A full house or four-of-a-kind receive the same payout, while pure royal flushes and royal flushes featuring a wild card have a massive difference in payout; 100 credits for a wild royal flush, and 4,000 credits for a pure royal flush. Should you hit the second-best hand possible (four-of-a-kind wild deuces), you can expect a return of $258.75 for a $1.25 bet!

Hand	Pays
Royal flush no deuces	4,000
Four deuces	1,000
Royal flush with deuce	100
Five-of-a-kind	60
Straight flush	50
Four-of-a-kind	20
Full house	20
Flush	15
Straight	10
Three-of-a-kind	5

Four deuces on a wild-card machine is second only to a royal flush

What are you playing for?

Your approach to a video poker machine should be tempered by your goal. If you want to amuse yourself while you're having a break from more serious gambling, there's little point sitting at a machine that is geared to paying out good odds for monster hands but ignores everything below three-of-a-kind. Machines featuring wild cards, such as Deuces Wild and Joker Poker, are lots of fun because of the number of hands you can form, but you'll consequently get much weaker odds. Fortunately, most machines placed in casinos offer multiple games (some even offer the diversion of video Blackjack) so you can sit at one console and switch between games whenever you want.

Strategies

Video poker is a volatile game where you might lose for long periods of time, or just get your stake back. Because you have one round in which to make discards, strategy comes into play more than, say, on a slot machine. The key to success on video poker machines is to discard in a way that gives you the highest expectation of winning. Often you might have to sacrifice a made pair in order to chase down a more profitable hand, such as a flush or straight. To expect to make money on video poker, you first have to accept that your ambitions should be tailored to a long-run game, not a quick-hit return.

If you're used to playing poker you might look at a screen of 8-4-J-K-2 and hold the Jack and King. However, you're going to get much better odds-wise to hold only one of them. To draw four cards in an attempt to make a single pair is much better than holding two. The odds are against you hitting two pairs, and you effectively waste one of your drawing cards to at least complete one pair and have your money returned on an evens payout.

Play maximum credits

If you plan to take video poker seriously, you must always play the maximum credits allowed to access the higher payout schedules. You would be better off playing at a cheaper machine if that allows your bankroll to cover the five-credit maximum bet.

Even though you can only expect to hit a jackpot hand (i.e. the full royal flush) once every 30,000 or 40,000 hands, it still pays enough to make this a large part of your expected return.

Always go for a royal flush

Some things don't change and the hand you really want to see on a video poker machine is a royal flush. Hit one of these and you'll be on champagne for the rest of the night. The bad news is that they're as rare round the bar as they are in the card room. What you need to do is maximize your chances of hitting one, which means occasionally dropping premium hands in the quest for the royal. This might go against your conservative nature, but if you want to win big, it's an essential strategy.

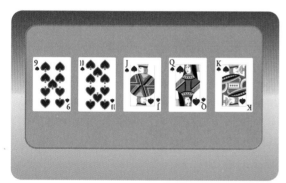

9s-10s-Js-Qs-Ks

Get dealt this hand and you'd be forgiven for jumping out of your seat and doing a little dance. However, following our advice you're going to have to break up this party and sacrifice the 9s in an attempt to hit the Ace of spades. Though it might seem madness to break up a made hand, you're currently guaranteed to win 250 credits for your five-credit bet. If you were to make the royal flush you'd win 4,000 credits for your five-credit bet.

Example:

If a single credit were 25c, a five-credit bet is $1.25
To hit a straight flush = $62.50
To improve to a royal flush = $1,000
If a single credit were $1, a five-credit bet would = $5
To hit a straight flush = $250
To improve to a royal flush = $4,000

Obviously this is where you find out how much of a gambler you are. Would you rather stand pat (i.e. hold them all) and take a smaller guaranteed amount, or risk losing that amount to have a chance at making a real profit? If you ever have the choice between drawing one card to make a flush or two cards to make a royal flush, you should always go for the royal flush because of the increased payback.

Wild-card strategies

Playing video poker games that feature wild cards can ultimately bend some of the rules of poker drawing that you've learnt. Straights and flushes become far easier to achieve because the wild cards in the deck increase your number of outs dramatically. At the same time the odds drop dramatically.

If you're ever dealt two wild deuces, always roll all other cards, even if you've made a wild flush or straight. Although it's tempting to stick with a made hand (accepting that you will more often than not end up with an inferior three-of-a-kind) the opportunity to make a deuces four-of-a-kind is too valuable to miss.

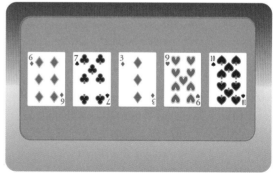

6-7-3-9-10

If this were a standard Jacks or Better game you would be better advised to draw all five cards again than hold the 6-7-9 and 10 in the hope of hitting one of your four outs (i.e. an 8 to complete the straight). In a game featuring wild cards, your number of outs doubles, so it becomes a profitable play to go for the gutshot draw.

3s-7s-7h-10s-2d
With only three spades showing in a game with no wild cards, holding the spades and hoping to hit two more would be a bad move. With a wild-card game it's much more profitable as you now effectively have 14 outs to hit (the 10 spades left in the deck, plus four wild cards).

7s-2h-8s-9s-Kd
This hand has an even higher positive expectation. Holding the three spades now leaves you with 14 outs for the flush, but also a great number of outs to complete a straight.

Is it fixed?

A lot of people are extremely suspicious of machines like this, but the good news is that they're heavily regulated and all are required by law to offer an entirely random shuffle. Any shuffling machine is required to have the same odds as a random manual shuffle would.

Flexing your poker skills

Being a seasoned poker player you will have no doubt honed your skills and have a certain feel for poker hands, their likeliness, and just what is and

TIP

If you plan to spend even a small amount of time playing video poker in any casino, be sure to join one of their loyalty schemes. They're free and, though you might not think you're a hardened enough gambler to make this worthwhile, you might just be eligible for a freebie such as a casino T-shirt or mug. With enough play, you might even get a free lunch!

isn't worth chasing. The good news is that most of your general poker know-how will translate well to video poker. For example, drawing two cards in the hope of hitting a flush is just as unlikely to work in video poker as it is in a normal game of draw poker. There are, however, a few mental changes that you need to make:

Aces are no longer the best card you can be dealt. The best card now is actually any card that can pair up and get you paid. If you're playing a game of Jacks or Better, a pair of Jacks is as good as a pair of Kings or Aces.

8-J-J-2-3
A pair of Jacks wins just as much as a pair of Aces.

The lowest card that qualifies to make a pair now becomes the more powerful card because it also has more possibilities to be part of a straight than an Ace does.

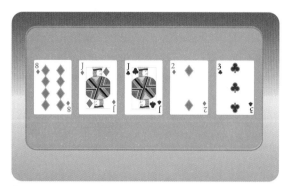

8-J-J-2-3
The lowest card that qualifies to make a pair now becomes the more powerful card because it also has more possibilities to be part of a straight than an Ace does.

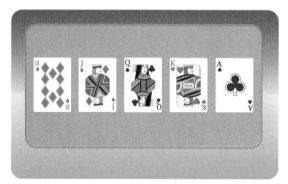

10-J-Q-K-A
The only straight an Ace can complete is an Ace-high straight.

7-8-9-10-J, 8-9-10-J-Q, 9-10-J-Q-K, 10-J-Q-K-A
The Jack is much more powerful here (assuming you are playing a Jacks or Better machine) because it can complete four different straight configurations, and score in a pair.

Understanding variance

Put simply, variance refers to how choppy your game will be – how high are the highs, and how low are the lows. If you play a basic version of video poker without wild cards and bonus payout structures, you can expect a reasonably smooth ride. Though you are less likely to see big hands, you will still get paid off for the lowest-ranking hands. This sort of game is good if you've got a small bankroll, and you want it to last a while.

A game that doesn't pay the lower hands and uses wild cards has much more variance. You could find yourself plummeting to the limits of your bankroll, followed by a run of big wins that puts you back ahead again. If you enjoy rollercoaster rides, this is your game.

Other types of video poker

There are lots of other types of video poker, some aimed at players looking for entertainment, and some that make the game more exciting without substantially adding to the risk or reward.

Novelty video poker games are abundant and varied. Movie licensces, TV game shows and cultural icons have all been plundered to offer the player something more interesting to look at. Generally they are nothing more than the standard machines you've already read about, but with more amusing and interesting graphics and sounds. Make sure you check the payouts before you're lured in by the flashing lights though.

TIP

Avoid machines that offer the same payback for two pairs as they do for a single pair. Two pairs should account for approximately 25 per cent of your total returns, so these machines give an extra 12 per cent back to the house, but don't compensate equally with the higher payouts on larger hands.

Multi-hand games

Multi-hand games offer you the chance to play your hand across a number of mirrored cards. Though you're initially dealt one hand as per normal video poker, once you decide which cards to exchange your selection is mirrored across a multitude of hands displayed on the screen. This might only be one additional hand, or it could be anything up to 50 or even 100. This is only limited by the individual machine you're playing and how many hands you've paid for at the cost of one extra credit a time. Have you got deep pockets?

Multi-hand video poker

Though you're paying one extra credit for each additional hand, you might receive more than that outlay in return if good cards improve across the various live hands. By deciding to hold the two Kings in this example, the Kings are mirrored across all the hands that you've paid a credit for. This gives you a chance to improve on all of them.

Success!

You don't improve on your main hand, but on two of the other mirrors you improve to three-of-a-kind, on another two you hit two-pair and one of the hands improves to a full house. As you spent 10 times more for these additional hands, you obviously need to improve on the majority of hands beyond even money to make it profitable.

Slot poker

As poker becomes more and more popular, slots are starting to cash in. Spin Poker is just one example. Using the standard slot configuration, each credit you spend buys you another win line. As well as horizontal win lines across the screen, diagonal, symmetrical, and weird and wacky win lines eventually fill the screen if you commit enough credits. Besides buying these multiple win lines, the lines can be pumped with more than just one bet to increase the return that each win line delivers. Should you actually make some big hands, a bewildering visual show kicks off as the various hands you've made across the screen come to life, one by one. Remember though that slots can drain your pockets.

Checklist

- Video poker can be a fun diversion from the card room

- Even though you're playing against the house you can find machines with a pretty healthy return

- Machines with wild cards increase the number of big hands you'll hit

- But they also reduce the payouts you'll get

- Remember that if you're playing video poker you'll get a few free drinks from the casino. It's the least you deserve

If you want to play a slot machine, make it one based on poker.

Table Games

1

'Remember this: the house doesn't beat the player. It just gives him the opportunity to beat himself.'
NICK 'THE GREEK' DANDALOS (Professional Gambler)

Honeymoon in Vegas: Nicolas Cage found Vegas a tough place. Learn how to play table games and you'll have an easier ride

In this chapter you'll learn...

That poker's popularity has inevitably led to a rise in poker-based table games where you play against the casino and its house edge. They're still a lot of fun though and if you're looking for an instant hit you might as well give yourself the best chance of winning possible.

Table Games

Sick of chucking good money at the roulette table? Most casinos offer a variety of poker-based table games that can provide a fun diversion from the card-room. Just don't expect to beat the house.

One of the main reasons that casinos don't like poker is that it's a game that doesn't offer them an edge. And casinos don't like gambling unless they've got favourable odds. That's why they offer poker-based games on the main gaming floor.

Caribbean Stud Poker

As with all table games, though there may be from 2-9 players at any one table, you play your hand against the dealer, and you never compete directly with the other players. Caribbean Stud is probably the simplest of the table poker games, and one that you're likely to pick up quickly.

Sequence of play

Each player indicates the desire to play by placing a bet in the ante mark on the table. This amount must be within the limit displayed on the table, and it represents the minimum you'll lose as well as the maximum you can bet later in the game. Once all live players have placed their ante, the dealer deals each player five face-down cards in turn, and then five cards to himself, exposing the last card in the sequence.

Each player must now look at his hand and decide if he wishes to continue in the round. Any players wishing to fold place their cards face-down over the raise area of the table. These cards will be collected by the dealer, along with the players' original antes.

It might not be an equal playing field but you can still have a lot of fun taking on the casino

If you want to continue in the round you have to put double your original ante in the raise area of the table. So, if you started off with the minimum $5 bet, you can only put $10 into the raise area. This means that if you want to minimize your losses by betting the lowest allowed amount in the ante area, you're also crippling your ability to make larger

Caribbean Stud

Stud bet

With a bet made in the ante area you are recognized as a live player and dealt five cards accordingly. Any other live players will receive their cards, with the dealer taking five cards last. One of the dealer's cards will be revealed face-up.

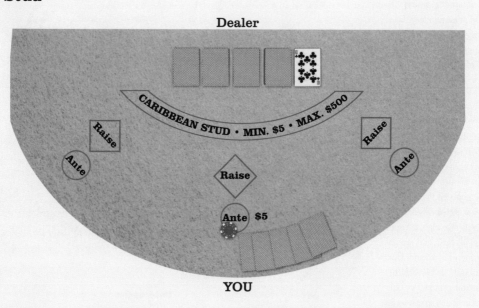

Stud raise

Though your cards are hidden from everyone else at this point, you can see that you hold a strong hand – a pair of Queens. As this is a hand worth playing, you indicate this by making a bet into the raise area. As your initial ante was $5, your raise can only be double this ante – thus your bet is $10.

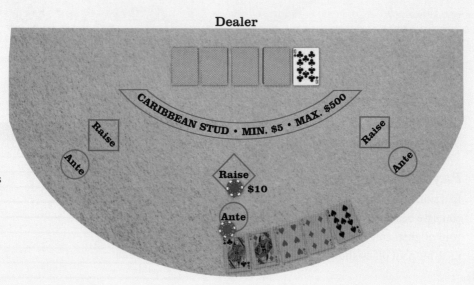

Stud – non-qualifying

In this first illustration we'll show what happens when the dealer fails to qualify. The dealer needs to show at least Ace-King to play, and in this instance he has failed to make this minimum requirement. When this happens, regardless of your hand, your initial ante is paid off at even money (i.e. the amount you anted is matched), and your raise is returned.

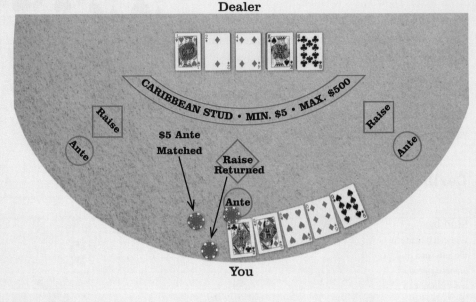

Stud – qualifying

In this example the dealer has qualified with a pair of tens so you get to compete with him for the best hand. If the dealer's hand is the best, you lose your ante and your raise. Here, your two pairs are good against his Tens, and you get your ante matched and your raise paid off at the odds for your winning hand. Two pair gets paid at 2-1, so you receive $5 for your original $5 ante, plus $20 for your $10 raise. A $30 profit for $15 staked. Well done!

amounts if you're dealt a strong hand. Balance and control is a necessary skill in Caribbean Stud!

Payout odds

In a situation where the dealer has qualified and you have beaten him in the hand, as well as seeing your original ante matched, you will have your raise bet paid off as shown here...

Hand	Odds
A-K/one pair	1-1
Two-pair	2-1
Three-of-a-kind	3-1
Straight	4-1
Flush	5-1
Full house	7-1
Four-of-a-kind	20-1
Straight flush	50-1
Royal flush	100-1

Strategy

Though this is mostly a game of luck (either you get dealt a good hand or you don't), there is one area of the game which you can influence, and that's whether to post a raise regardless of the hand you hold in the hope that the dealer doesn't qualify. The fact that the dealer shows one of his cards means that you do at least have some information to act upon. If the dealer already shows an Ace or King, you know that the chances of him qualifying have just leapt up. Whether you choose to risk doubling the ante to protect your initial stake is up to you.

Guidelines

Feel free to gamble as you want, but the following basic guidelines will statistically serve you well.

- Raise with any pair.
- Raise with A-K-Q-J-x (x being any random fifth card).
- Raise when holding A-K and a high card at least matching the dealer's upcard.
- Fold if you have less than the dealer's qualifying hand (i.e. A-K).

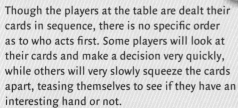

Advanced

Though the players at the table are dealt their cards in sequence, there is no specific order as to who acts first. Some players will look at their cards and make a decision very quickly, while others will very slowly squeeze the cards apart, teasing themselves to see if they have an interesting hand or not.

If you wait until last to act, you can see how many players at the table choose to raise their ante and continue in the hand. Though you can only learn over time what kinds of hands your specific table is playing, it wouldn't be crazy to assume that the player choosing to continue betting has at least A-K or better. And the more players that indicate this, the less likely it is the dealer has A-K or better. It's not an exact science, but it can give you a slight edge.

Progressive side bets

Many of the table games you encounter on the casino floor will feature a progressive jackpot. This means that a number of tables are linked together, and feature a flashing total jackpot that increases as more time and play passes. You will often see an additional coin slot by the ante and raise area, or an extra plate that detects the metal coins that the dealers will furnish you with if you want to play the progressive option. By placing a coin here at the same time you enter the ante, you become eligible for the progressive jackpots. Typically, certain hands are paid a set amount, while other hands (generally the very rare hands) are paid out a percentage of the progressive bonus amount.

On a $5 table you could expect to receive...

100 per cent of the progressive jackpot for a royal flush.

10 per cent of the progressive jackpot for a straight flush.

1 per cent of the progressive jackpot for four-of-a-kind.

$150 for a full house.

$75 for a flush.

$50 for a straight.

Pai Gow Poker

Traditionally an Asian game played with domino-like tiles, the westernized version of Pai Gow Poker features a 52-card deck and one Joker that can act as a wild card to complete a straight, a flush, or a straight flush. It's a more complicated table game and at first glance it might look indeciperable, but once you know what you're doing it's a lot of fun.

Once you've placed your bet, you're dealt seven cards which must then be split into two hands – one five-card hand, and one two-card hand. The five-card hand must be the stronger of the two hands. If you mistakenly make a stronger two-card hand, you automatically lose as the hand is considered a foul.

Once you've split your hand, you place the two hands on to the table and the dealer takes his turn. Once the dealer reveals his five-card and two-card hand, it is compared to yours. If you beat the dealer on both hands, you win. If the dealer beats you on both hands, you lose. Otherwise it's a push (i.e. a draw). If you have an absolute tie (e.g. both you and the dealer show A-9), then the house wins. Because of the

Advanced!

When the dealer first deals out the seven-card starting hands, he will then roll a die to decide who gets which batches of cards. This is an act of ritual and not something you should worry about. The house also takes a commission from winning bets. Again, leave this to your dealer to sort out. They are all being watched very closely so you don't need to worry about any mistakes ruining your profit!

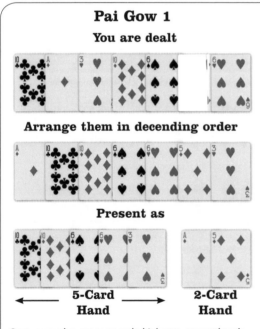

Pai Gow 1
You are dealt

Arrange them in decending order

Present as

5-Card Hand ← → 2-Card Hand

Once you receive your seven cards, it's best to arrange them in descending order to make splitting easier. Remember that you must have a stronger five-card hand than your two-card hand. An option here would be to play the pair of Sixes as your two-card hand, but as the Ace-high is a strong enough two-card hand – and a single pair of Tens not so strong as a five-card hand – you're better off going for two-pair on your five-card hand.

Pai Gow 2
You are dealt

Arrange them as

Present as

5-Card Hand ← → 2-Card Hand

Here you can use the Joker as a 3 to complete a straight from 2-6. The Joker can only be used to complete a straight, a flush, or a straight flush.

Advanced!

You can also opt to play as the Bank – winning all ties and the five per cent commission charged after losses are set against winnings. If you opt to play as the Bank, you must have enough money in front of you to pay off all winning bets to the other players and dealer. The option to play as the Bank is offered to each player in turn.

amount of pushes that you see in Pai Gow Poker, this is a fun game to play and a small bankroll can last a long time. Like the other table games Pai Gow Poker is also a very friendly game to play. Unlike the poker table proper, you're not competing against your fellow players. Instead you're all on the same side and a community win can be celebrated noisily.

Pai Gow win

Dealer shows

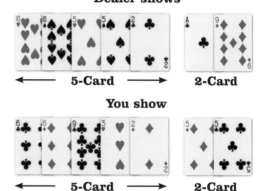

You show

Here you beat the dealer's five-card pair of Tens with your trip Eights, and you beat the dealer's two-card Ace/Queen with your pair of Sixes.

Pai Gow push

Dealer shows

You show

Here the dealer beats your 5-card single pair with two pair, while your 2-card pair of Fives beats his Ace-high. This is a push, and your initial bet is returned to you.

Pai Gow lose

Dealer shows

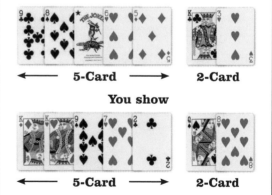

You show

Here the dealer's straight beats your pair of Kings in the five-card hand, while his King-high beats your Queen-high in the two-card hand. You lose.

TIP

The only way you can influence the game is by selecting which cards will make the strongest two-card hand, and which one will make the strongest five-card hand. If you're ever unsure, you can expose your cards to the dealer who will tell you how the house would set it. As you act before the dealer, there's no way that the dealer can use this situation to his advantage.

Let It Ride

A familiar table in casinos since 1993, Let It Ride is very popular due to its simplicity. You begin by placing a bet in each of the three betting circles on the table's layout. Most casinos will have a minimum bet of $5 so you are potentially betting a minimum of $15 on each hand. There may also be a $1 bonus bet option that sits beside the three main betting circles. A bet here receives a set pay-off should you hit a specific hand. More on that in a moment...

Once the three mandatory bets have been placed, each player receives three cards in turn. The dealer will then deal himself two cards that remain face-down in front of him. Ultimately these two cards will be revealed, and will be used with your three cards to make the best 5-card poker hand.

At this stage you can now look at your cards and decide upon your next action. When the

Let It Ride is one of the easiest table games to play

dealer comes to you in sequence you can either take back the first of your bets from the first betting circle (often indicated by making a dragging movement with your cards against the table in front of this bet), or let it ride by leaving the bet untouched. Once the dealer has attended to all the players, one of his cards is revealed.

There is now a second circuit of the table, with each player again having the option to take back their bet, or to let it ride. After this round, the dealer will reveal his final card, and all players can see the five cards (three of their own and the dealer's two) that will make up their final hand. The third bet made by the player cannot be taken back, so essentially the game has a minimum of a single bet, and a maximum of three bets. The dealer will then work round the players, examining their final 5-card hand and paying out or raking in their bets accordingly.

Payout

Below is an example of the typical payout schedule you'll encounter on Let It Ride tables.

Hand	Payout
Pair of 10s or better	1-1
Two pair	2-1
Three-of-a-kind	3-1
Straight	5-1
Flush	8-1
Full house	11-1
Four-of-a-kind	50-1
Straight flush	200-1
Royal flush	1,000-1

WARNING!

As this is a game where 40 per cent of your ultimate hand is hidden, you're not allowed to communicate with other players. If you knew the other hands in play you'd have information that could potentially give you an edge over the casino.

Strategy

Though Let It Ride is a very simple game, there is some basic strategy to be employed to ensure a worthwhile risk versus reward payout.

• **Bet # 1.** Let It Ride when you hold a pair of Tens or better, three cards to a royal flush or straight flush.

• **Bet # 2.** Let It Ride when you hold a pair of Tens or better, four cards to a royal or straight flush or flush, four high cards (10 and above) or an open-ended straight.

//////////////////////////////
WARNING!
All table games are played against the house and ultimately the house edge. Treat them as a fun diversion but accept that, in the long run, you're battling against the odds.

//////////////////////////////

Bonus payout

As mentioned, many of the Let It Ride tables you'll encounter offer a $1 bonus bet. By entering $1 into this side bet, you become eligible for a bonus payout should you complete any specific 5-card poker hands from three-of-a-kind upwards. Though this amount varies, the details below give you an idea of a typical payout structure. And remember that if you're lucky enough to get a royal flush you'll really regret not having put that extra dollar down.

Hand	Payout
Three-of-a-kind	$5
Straight	$25
Flush	$50
Full house	$200
Four-of-a-kind	$400
Straight flush	$3,000
Royal flush	$30,000

Let It Ride

The basic layout of the Let It Ride table. In front of each player there are three places to make a bet that must be between the table minimum and maximum. You might also see a slot or plate for a bonus bet. The player receives three cards, and the dealer takes two cards. In the first and second round of the game, each player may choose to take back their bet or let it ride.

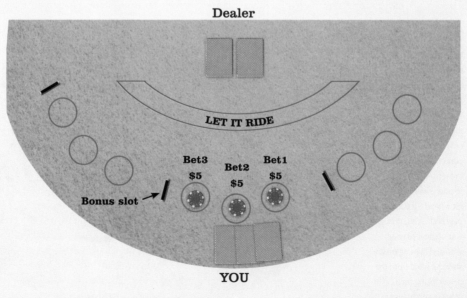

Three-card Poker

Another of the simplest table games you'll find in the casino, Three-card Poker is extremely popular and great fun. The game itself is actually two separate games running at the same time – PairPlus and Ante and Play. To start, you place a bet on either one or both of these spots on the table in amounts governed only by the minimum/maximum table stake advertised. Both of these hands are based upon the three-card poker hands you receive.

PairPlus

This part of Three-card Poker is very simple, and is not actually played against the dealer. A bet in the PairPlus box will return a payout as detailed below, should the three-card hand contain one of the standard poker hands.

Hand	Payout
Pair	1-1
Flush	4-1
Straight	6-1
Three-of-a-kind	30-1
Straight flush	40-1

Ante and Play

This is the part of the game that is played against the dealer's own three-card hand. Having placed a wager in the ante area and examined your cards, you can choose to fold – losing your ante and the PairPlus bet – or raise by placing an equal amount to the ante in the raise area of the table. Once you have indicated a raise you are up against the dealer. The dealer must show at least Queen-high to qualify.

Outcome and payout
- If the dealer doesn't qualify, the ante wins 1-1, and the raise is returned.
- If the dealer qualifies and beats the player, both the ante and raise are lost.
- If the dealer qualifies and ties the player, both the ante and raise are pushed.
- If the dealer qualifies and the player beats him, both the ante and raise win 1-1.

Ante bonus

Regardless of the dealer's hand, there are also bonus odds that affect the ante bet. Should you

Three-card poker

Here you can see the basic layout, with the ante area, the raise area, and the PlayPlus area. You can choose to only play the PairPlus, or only the Ante and Play part of the game, but the returns are much greater – when you do hit a hand – if you opt to play both. Also, though you might lose your ante and raise against a stronger hand from the dealer, being paid off in PairPlus might lessen your losses.

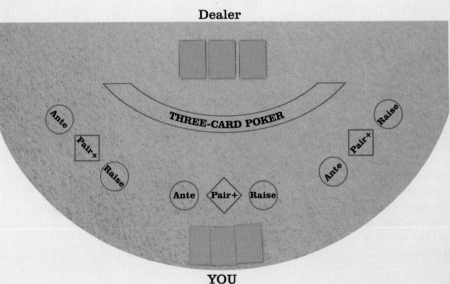

Three-card poker

Here, regardless of the dealer's hand, you instantly receive 1-1 for making a pair on PairPlus. As you entered a raise, you also compete against the dealer. Here you beat his King-high (remembering the dealer only needs to show Queen-high to qualify) with a pair of Aces. Both your ante and your raise bet get paid off at 1-1.

Here your flush has been beaten by the dealer's straight, losing you your ante and raise. However, because you made a bet on the PairPlus area, you receive 4-1 for that bet.

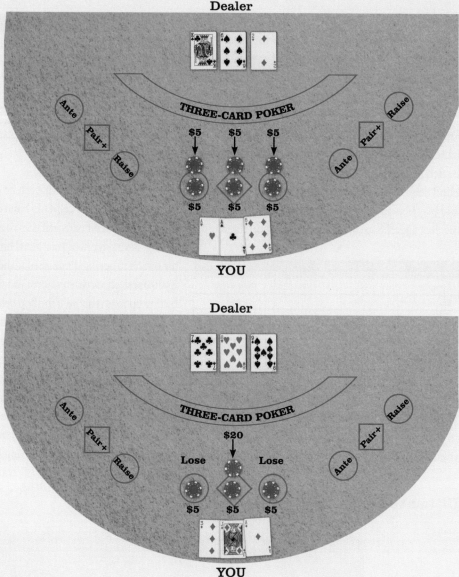

show three-of-a-kind, you receive 4-1 on your ante. Show a straight flush and you'll receive 5-1. Obviously, if you are playing both PairPlus and Ante and Play, when you do hit a hand, the returns are much better.

Ultimate Texas Hold'em

The global popularity of Hold'em has resulted in a number of new table games and, if you're after a quick fix and can't commit to the card room, this is an excellent alternative. The most popular of the current crop of games is Ultimate Texas Hold'em.

You begin by making an equal bet in the ante and blind area and then receive two cards. Once you've seen your cards you can make a bet of either 3x or 4x your ante in the play area, or check. The dealer then deals the flop. If you've not already bet you can now bet 2x your ante, at which point the dealer reveals the last two community cards. Now you have to either fold or make a bet at least 1x the ante.

If you stay in the hand until the end, your hand is compared to the dealer's, who must show at least a pair to qualify. If the dealer doesn't qualify the ante bets are returned to the player, while all other bets are paid off. If you and the dealer show the same hand, it's a push and all bets are returned. If you're beaten by the dealer, you lose the play, ante and blind bets. If you beat the dealer, you get your ante and play bets matched at even money. The blind bet receives specific payouts dependent upon the hand.

Hand	Payout
Straight	1-1
Flush	3-2
Full house	3-1
Four-of-a-kind	10-1
Straight flush	50-1
Royal flush	5001

There is also a separate spot on the table called trips. This is an optional bonus bet that you're free to make on every round. If you hit a specific hand, you'll receive a payout as per the following schedule.

Hand	Payout
Three-of-a-kind	3-1
Straight	5-1
Flush	6-1
Full house	8-1
Four-of-a-kind	30-1
Straight flush	40-1
Royal flush	50-1

Strategy

There is very little strategy that can be employed with this game (either the deck delivers a hand or it doesn't), but a basic knowledge of odds will help you decide whether to bet big, having received your initial hole cards, or not. As the option to bet big diminishes as the hand progresses, if you opt to check when you're dealt 6-8, you'll have your betting options reduced if the flop delivers 7-9-10.

A seasoned Hold'em player will know which starting hands have a strong possibility of developing into a winning hand, but will also know how easily a flop can destroy a winning hand. The trips bonus area provides a certain amount of consolation because (should you hit a good hand but find it beaten by the dealer) you will at least receive monies against that hand, regardless of you winning or losing in the showdown.

Ultimate Texas Hold'em

Dealer

ULTIMATE TEXAS HOLD'EM

Trips $5
Ante $5 = Blind $5
Play $5

You

It's the closest game to poker that you'll find on the table floor and for that reason alone we'd recommend giving it a whirl.

Checklist

- There's much more to casino games than first meets the eye

- Use them as a quick fix if you're short on time

- Playing them will net you the minimum of a few free drinks...

- But with a little strategy you can vastly increase your return

- Understanding which game suits your goals best is paramount...

- But ultimately you have to treat them as a fun diversion and expect to lose

Treat table games as a fun diversion and nothing more and you'll have a good time

Poker Etiquette

'It's easy to be a tough competitor and still be the kind of person with whom people love to compete.'
CHUCK THOMPSON (Professional Poker Player)

In this chapter you'll learn...

How to conduct yourself while playing poker. It's like going to finishing school, and remember that, even if you're not the best player in the world you can be the best behaved, and that's another way of earning respect from other players.

Wear what you want to the table, but make sure you're well behaved

Poker Etiquette

Like any other game poker comes with its own set of rules – spoken and unspoken. They're not hard to learn though and in this chapter we're going to show you how to act like a pro at the table.

Poker, like any other game, comes with a set of rules that are stringently adhered to. So, in Texas Hold'em, everyone gets two cards; you always get a flop, turn and river to make up your hand, and the highest hand always wins. But there are lots of other 'rules' covering etiquette that occupy a grey area. Breaking them might not get you chucked out of a game, but they could incur penalties and anger fellow players.

First, remember that poker is a social game, even on the Internet. And because you're playing with other people you're supposed to behave with a certain decorum ensuring that, win or lose,

Mike 'The Mouth' Matusow is one of the best poker players in the world. He's not the best behaved

everyone has a good time. And ultimately that's what everyone wants, especially when you're winning. You want the losers to come back to your table and drop their wallets into your lap again and again and again.

To make it easy, we've broken poker etiquette down into 13 easy steps. Whether you follow all or some of them is up to you, and will obviously depend on whether you're playing with friends or strangers.

· Read this book
Most poker players are gentle with beginners as long as they're willing to pick things up quickly. You don't have to be an expert in every nuance, but it's important that you know the basics. If you've read this book from cover to cover you should know enough to get by.

· Post your blinds
Blinds are the forced bets designed to kick-start the action at the beginning of every hand. Try to remember when it's your turn to post them (i.e. when you're one of the two players to the left of the dealer, known as the small and big blind respectively) as it can be extremely annoying for the other players, or the dealer, to have to remind you every time it's your turn. And it slows down the game.

· Don't splash the pot
Splashing the pot is when you throw chips into the pile on the table. Why is that wrong? It makes

TRIVIA!

There's a famous scene in the excellent poker-based film *Rounders*, where Matt Damon's character tells Teddy KGB not to splash the pot. The reply is fairly ripe, 'In my club I will splash the pot whenever I like', with a big expletive thrown in for good measure. The moral? Etiquette goes out of the window if you're playing the boss. And if you're the boss, you can do what you like.

Watch *Rounders* – it's a classic poker film

it a lot harder for the dealer, or anyone else on the table, to see what you've bet and it's considered extremely rude. You don't have to place your chips carefully over the line (although you can if you want); you can slide them, chuck them, whatever. Just make sure that they remain separate from the other piles of chips on the table.

· Act in turn

Poker is a betting game, and if you don't act in turn you're giving information away to other players on the table still to bet. And this is going to send any players who have already posted their bets ballistic.

Let's explain. There are three people left to bid, Player A, yourself and Player B. Player A is just about to fold when you, because you're not paying attention, muck your hand out of turn. Player A now has to consider his options. His hand might not have been good enough to take on two people (yourself and Player B), but he's extremely happy to chance his arm against one opponent. He puts in a decent raise and Player B is forced to fold, although not before fixing you with his patent death stare.

And it can also work against you. If you bet out of turn, perhaps because you've got an amazing hand and you just can't wait, then you might persuade others who should be bidding next to fold, losing you a fair chunk of the pot. And if your bet is allowed to stand unchallenged, you might lose the right to raise the pot if someone bets before you. So keep your eye on the game and, if you do get lost, see where the dealer button is because that'll tell you who was the first to bet. If you're still none the wiser, just ask. No one will mind. And if you do act out of turn (it happens to the best), just hold your hands up and *apologize*. As long as you don't make a habit of it, most players will accept an honest mistake.

· Keep schtum

However tempting it might be to let your opponents know what you folded with when the flop is revealed, don't do it because you're giving those left vital information that could change the result of the game.

For example, three hearts come down on the flop and you can't help exclaiming that you folded the Ace of Hearts. If someone still playing has a King-high flush, then he knows he's now holding the nuts. So keep quiet until the hand is over. And that also goes for giving advice, even if someone asks for it. You'll make them angry if you're wrong, and you'll make their opponent angry if you're right. But whatever you do, don't show your cards to the table when you fold while the hand is still in play. In fact you shouldn't ever show cards but, if you have to, wait until the hand has finished and then abide by the 'show one show all' rule (below).

· Show one, show all

We'd advise you never to show your cards to your opponents because you're just giving them information for free. If you can't resist the temptation (and some players actually like to feed information to their opponents deliberately in order to trap them later), it's accepted that if you show one person then you should show everyone at the table. The dealer should enforce this (and if you're playing online you have no choice); the best solution is to place them face-up.

· Watch the time

It's currently a hot topic in poker. If you're playing online you have a timer (usually 30 seconds) that lets you know exactly how much time you've got to make your decision before your hand is folded automatically (or checked if there has been no action before you). But that doesn't apply in live poker (unless you're playing in a speed poker tournament) – in fact there's no set time limit, and no definition of what a reasonable amount of time is. Some players deliberately exploit this to unsettle other players. Imagine that Player X takes about 10 minutes on each hand, pondering his options, then ponders some more before finally mucking his cards. The chances are he won't have a good hand every time, so he's actually sitting on garbage and knows he's going to fold instantly, but is taking his time in an attempt to put other players off their game.

But it's not just an off-putting tactic. If you're playing in a tournament with blinds that go up regularly – say every hour – a player that takes an age to act on every hand is going to seriously reduce the number of hands you see in each level, and that gives the other tables in play a big advantage.

You can call 'time' on another player by asking the dealer to put the clock on the player, but there's no set amount of time before you can do this. And most players don't think it should be their responsibility as it can cause a lot of bad blood. Players generally don't like being rushed. So, if you're faced with a heart-wrenching decision then take as long as you feel is necessary to make the right decision. If you've been acting punctually throughout the game then your opponents should respect you. If you've been tardy throughout, don't expect the same understanding. But don't sit there for 10 minutes with 7-3 off-suit, when you know you're going to fold, just to irritate your opponents. You're better than that.

· No mobile phones

In major tournaments mobile phones are banned and will earn you a suspension from the table, and possibly even disqualification from the entire tournament as you could be receiving information from someone who can see your opponent's cards. Even in the most casual home game they should be switched off. There's nothing more annoying than an excellent game of poker being broken up by a few minutes of platitudes to your partner. 'I'll be back soon. Yes, I know. I KNOW.' Do everyone a favour and switch it off.

· Mind your language

What's acceptable language for you may not be acceptable to others so, if you're playing with strangers, be thoughtful. They don't even like

> **TRIVIA!**
>
> If you're the sort of player who can't bear tardiness you might want to check out the new Speed Poker format that's quickly gaining in popularity. Instead of leaving it up to the players to decide the time limits, speed poker gives you 15 seconds to make your decision. If you can't do it in time, tough. Your hand will be checked or folded.

Speed Poker gives you just 15 seconds to make a decision, and it's proving popular with the new breed of Internet players

swearing at the table in the USA, where pretty much anything goes. In fact in major tournaments like the WSOP, swearing at the table can bring you a time suspension of 10 minutes and the penalty acts cumulatively. Mike Matusow found this out in the 2005 tournament, when he earned himself a 40-minute penalty for repeated infractions. If you're playing at home with your mates do whatever you normally do.

· **Be a good winner...**
When you win (and after you've read this book, you will), remember that someone else has lost. Crazy football-like celebrations are becoming more and more commonplace in poker but a lot of players find them distasteful. Imagine that you're on the end of the following hand. You've reached the heads-up (final two) stage of a big tournament and you've been dealt a pair of Aces. Short-stacked, you move all-in and, to your

delight, your opponent calls and reveals Ah-9s. You're well in charge, but the board unbelievably delivers him four hearts, giving him the nut flush on the river. Now what would you prefer him to do? Punch the air and then quickly shake your hand with a 'Well played'? Or ignore you and give everyone else in the room high-fives? Always remember, 'do unto others...' and you'll never go far wrong.

Mobile phones aren't welcome at the poker table, and could actually earn you a suspension or disqualification

If you win, someone else has lost. Try and remember that and leave the crazy celebrations until you've shaken his hand

· ... And take defeats with dignity

Don't be a bad loser. Accept it with grace, shrug your shoulders and congratulate the winner, even if he/she didn't play well. If you really can't bring yourself to say anything nice, don't say anything at all. Feel free to go back to your hotel room and bark at the moon if you've suffered a particularly bad beat. Just don't do it in public, or force your story on someone who's watching from the rail. They're really not interested in the manner in which you got your Aces cracked.

· Don't 'tap on the aquarium'

This one is for everyone's benefit. Bad poker players are known as fishes. And a good poker player wants as many fishes on their table as possible. So don't, whatever you do, scare off the bad players before you can take all their money. It might not sound nice but you're not playing poker to make friends. Say you're playing in a cash game with a couple of rich fish. They don't know how to play but they don't really care. They can afford to lose money and, as long as they're having a good time, they're more than happy to keep playing. Unfortunately,

one of the other players on the table thinks that it's his job to ridicule them. Every time one of them makes a bad play he points it out, making their lives a misery. Lo and behold they cut and run, with all their money. How do you feel towards the loudmouth? So if there are fish at the table, don't 'tap on the aquarium'. You'll scare them off.

· Unacceptable behaviour

Some etiquette rules are just there for guidance, but if you catch anyone acting violently, or in an inflammatory, sexist, racist or homophobic manner, get them chucked out of the game. If you're playing online report them to the management and get them banned for life.

· Do not covet your neighbour's ox

Oh hang on, that's a different book altogether. Mind you...

Above all, try and remember that poker's supposed to be fun. Use all of the points we've mentioned in this chapter for guidance and nothing else. We've got nothing against a bit of good-natured mischief on the poker table, and the poker world would be a pretty boring place if everyone was silent and sullen. Common sense should get you through but if you do manage to offend someone, apologize and shake their hand.

WARNING!

In some events swearing isn't just a breach of etiquette... At the WSOP and other major tournaments you're sin-binned for 10 minutes for swearing – it's called the F-Bomb rule – something Mike 'The Mouth' Matusow found out in the 2005 WSOP. He was banned for 40 minutes for repeatedly telling the dealer where to go.

TIP

Use your common sense. Winding people up at the table is seen by some as a legitimate tactic, especially in America. We're not saying that you should always be well behaved, but we're giving you the ground rules to use at your discretion. Treat others as you'd like them to treat you, and everything should be fine. Most of all, enjoy yourself, and if that means being a bit mischievous every now and again, well done.

Checklist

· **Learn the rules of the game**

· **Post your blinds promptly**

· **Don't splash the pot**

· **Act in turn**

· **Don't talk about hands until they're over**

· **If showing your cards, don't just show one player, show everyone**

· **Act in a reasonable time**

· **No mobile phones**

· **No bad language**

· **Be a good winner**

· **And take defeats with dignity**

· **Don't tap on the aquarium**

· **Use your common sense**

The Devilfish is the UK's best poker player and he's also one of the more colourful characters on the circuit. Don't expect him to stay quiet at the table

ultimatebet.com

25 Ways to Improve Your Game

'One day a chump, the next day a champion.
What a difference a day makes...'
MIKE SEXTON (Professional Poker Player)

In this chapter you'll learn...

To improve your play instantly by making the following
25 rules part of your everyday game. You might not like
the sound of some of them – and you're free to pick,
choose and discard depending on the level of game
you're playing – but implement them and you'll be a
better poker player. Guaranteed.

A climactic scene
from the poker
film *A Big Hand
for the Little Lady*

25 Ways to Improve Your Game

Are you having problems with your game? Are you looking for a quick fix? We've got 25 simple suggestions that could well make you a much better poker player overnight.

Concentrate

1

You don't kick a ball in a game of football and then look away and start thinking about what you're going to have for lunch, so don't do it in poker. Remember that things are happening all the time. Switch off for a second and you might miss a crucial piece of information from one of your opponents. Even if you fold, watch the other players like a hawk as they might give away something that'll be useful in a later hand. Watch them when the flop comes down, and study their reactions when the turn and river cards are dealt. Look out for their betting patterns and note any mannerisms that give their game away. Most importantly, watch your own cards and behaviour. They'll be watching you too.

Don't drink

2

If you're playing to win, abstain or stick to a couple of drinks. If you're an extremely tight player you might think that a barrel of beer will improve you, but it won't. Experiment – play a lengthy game and drink – and the next morning try and recall how you played. It's not pretty is it?

3

Don't fall in love with a bad starting hand

Unsurprisingly, gamblers are a superstitious bunch. And quite a few poker players have become irrevocably attached to a particular starting hand. Say you win a huge pot in Texas Hold'em with 4s-7s. Does that mean you should always play the hand? Absolutely not. It means you should remember that luck plays a big part in poker, and that you should only play it in the right situation.

4   Perfect your poker face

It's not easy to iron out any kinks in your mannerisms. How are you supposed to know that you splash your chips messily every time you try to bluff your opponents? How can you stop yourself stroking your nose, or blinking twice when you get good hole cards? But while you might not be able to eliminate all these signs, you can try to get rid of the most obvious ones. So how about perfecting a fixed expression which applies no matter what the cards are? Stare straight ahead if that works for you, but make sure you can do it all the time. And if you play with friends on a regular basis, arrange an amnesty every month where you all let each other know what's giving them away. It'll make you better players.

5   No fear

Show a weakness at poker and you'll be ruthlessly exploited. You mustn't be scared of betting all your chips and gambling everything on the turn of a card, even though you know that you could be sunk by a single piece of bad luck. If you're scared you'll be paralysed, and won't play well. Consider everything you've invested in a tournament or cash game as spent, gone and forgotten, and concentrate on the fat winnings.

Control your emotions   6

Lose control of a pinball table and a huge TILT sign starts flashing wildly. Your flippers won't work and you'll lose your ball. Lose control of your emotions at the poker table and the word TILT might as well start flashing on your forehead. Yes it can be a cruel game. Yes you might lose to a 1 in a 100 shot every now and again, but getting agitated and angry will only make things worse. Every good poker player is capable of taking the rough with the smooth and knows that, in the end, luck will even out.

7 Watch poker on TV

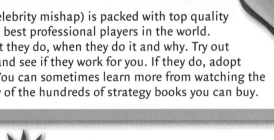

Each game (bar the odd celebrity mishap) is packed with top quality players, and very often the best professional players in the world. Watch them. Observe what they do, when they do it and why. Try out some of their techniques and see if they work for you. If they do, adopt them, if not, ditch them. You can sometimes learn more from watching the game on TV than from any of the hundreds of strategy books you can buy.

8 Play live, and on the Internet

Live poker and Internet poker are two radically different beasts and you might find that your natural game is better suited to one of them. Play both of them though and your overall game will be sharper. If you play live, start playing online even if it's just on the free tables. If you play almost exclusively online, then try a game at your local casino or arrange a regular game with your mates. You might find it hard to make the adjustment, and it might frustrate you at first, but it'll improve you because, whatever anyone says, there's no substitute for experience.

Be yourself 9

Everyone's got an opinion about how you should act at the poker table:

'Don't say a word'   'Don't wear shades'
'Be friendly and chatty'   'Stick your iPod on'
'Wear shades'   'Listen to everything
                               anyone says'

At the end of the day, everyone's got an opinion but there's no right or wrong, so do your own thing. If you want to wear a feather boa at the table, do it. If someone tells you that what you're doing is wrong, ignore them. Or tell them to mind their own business. Or turn the volume up on your iPod. Be yourself.

Learn how to riffle

OK, this isn't actually about improving your game and it's certainly not necessary, but note that when you sit down at a table and the person next to you starts riffling his chips, he's trying to intimidate you. He's telling you, in no uncertain terms, he's the daddy. So just give him a few minutes then show him one of the harder tricks, like the butterfly, and watch him shrink back into his kennel.

11 Bet like a pro

You don't want to be labelled a fish. A fish will instantly attract the attention of every other player on the table. And there's no better way to get the evil eye than to bet like an amateur. So, in the early stages of a sit-and-go, when you're dealt pocket Aces and the blinds are ridiculously low, don't go all-in pre-flop. Conversely, don't bet low all the way to the showdown and then turn over the nuts. People will laugh at you. Make decent-sized bets and don't fall into a pattern that's easy to spot.

Bluff selectively 12

There's no greater joy in poker than bluffing someone off a pot. But don't let it go to your head. Every decent player knows that you can't get good hands all the time, and if you bluff like a maniac people will know and they'll wait to trap you. Sure, be aggressive, but knowing when to bluff and when to switch gears and play premium hands is the art of a solid poker player.

13 Know your limits

Poker is one of the safest forms of gambling. Play tournaments and you know exactly what you're spending, and what you've got a chance of winning. Cash games are different, and you should only play with a sensible limit. Risk more than you can afford to lose and you'll be out of your 'safety zone', your confidence and play will suffer, and you'll lose more. It's a nasty cycle.

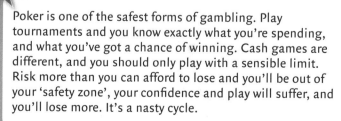

14 Practise heads-up

Playing heads-up or one-on-one is very different to playing poker with a number of people. It exemplifies the 'playing the player' side of the game, and it's much more aggressive and fast-paced. But if you've got any ambitions of winning this is a facet of your game that needs fine-tuning. It's like a football team practising penalties before the World Cup. And remember that you can always find heads-up opponents online if you can't dig out a willing partner in real life.

Know when to fold 'em 15

You might start with a good hand but, as the game develops, if you think you're beat, get out and cut your losses. You might have heard someone say, 'Well, I think I'm beat but I'm going to have to call you anyway.' Well no, actually, you don't. If you think you're beat, admit defeat.

16 Know your game

You might be a master of Texas Hold'em, but a switch to Omaha or seven-card Stud could bankrupt you in a matter of hours. There are loads of poker variants and although some only involve subtle rule switches, the differences in reality can be immense. Practise each game and make sure you know it inside out before you start playing for serious money.

Don't look at your cards 17

OK, you're going to have to look at your cards at some point, unless you've got a sixth sense (in which case you won't need this book), but don't do it before you have to. You can give away information when you peek at your cards, so why give your opponents the advantage of seeing your reaction before they've acted? And if you're looking at your cards out of turn, you're not looking where you should be looking – at your opponents looking at their hole cards. It might be tempting to snatch a look as soon as the cards have left the dealer's hand, but don't.

18 Be aggressive selectively

And we don't mean thumping someone if you don't like the way they play. Poker is a game that's won almost exclusively by aggressive betting. Play a meek, tight, passive game and you won't win regularly. You need to learn to switch gears and play much more aggressively in certain situations. There's no set way to do this, you'll need to adapt it to your own game over time, working out when and where it's appropriate.

Don't follow patterns 19

It's vital that you mix your play up as much as possible. If your opponent can see that you're playing to a set pattern then he'll be able to take money off you at will. Don't always raise with Aces, Kings or other premium hands. If you do this, then your opponent will be able to fold easily and he'll also know that if you just call he can push you off the pot with a big raise. And similarly don't always fold rags. Remember that you don't necessarily need the best hand in poker to win.

20 Learn the lingo

Poker can be extremely intimidating when you're not sure what people are talking about. Flop? River? Burn? Turn to page 182 and all will become clear.

21 Learn how to shuffle

If you play online your cards are shuffled for you. If you can afford the $10,000 entry fee to the World Series of Poker, your cards are shuffled for you. If you turn up at your local casino or invite your friends round for the night, you'll need to take your turn shuffling the deck. And nobody wants to look like a ham-fisted fool. If you've no idea how to do it, just put all the cards face down on the table and mix them up using both hands. This is one of the most effective ways of shuffling the deck.

22 Check your cards like a pro

Have you ever seen a professional poker player lift his hole cards off the table, hold them close to his chest and look at them before placing them back down? No? Well there's a very good reason. Lift your cards off the table and you're running the risk of showing them to your opponents, and that's one step away from giving them your credit card and PIN number. Leave them flat on the table and squeeze the corners up while shielding them from prying eyes. It looks a lot cooler.

23 Play nicely

There are rules of etiquette that govern poker (see page 164) and, while actual interpretations vary wildly depending on what sort of game you're playing and in which country, you should follow as many as possible. Nobody wants to play with a boor, and if you continually wind up other players they won't play with you again.

24 Be mentally prepared

If you don't feel like playing or you're in a foul mood, are ill, overtired or otherwise detached from your normal equilibrium, don't play. It's that simple.

25 Read this book again

Not now, unless you want to. Give it a few weeks, play a few games and then flick back through the pages. There might be something you missed first time around, or there might be something you didn't really understand that makes more sense now that you're more experienced.

Checklist

- Concentration is the key
- Don't play when you're drunk
- Don't fall in love with a lucky hand
- Develop a poker face and don't be scared
- Control your emotions
- Watch poker on TV and play as much as you can
- Be your own person
- Learn how to bet like a pro and riffle chips
- Bluff selectively
- Play within your means
- Practise heads-up
- Know when to fold losing hands
- Know the rules of the game you're playing inside out
- Be aggressive – selectively
- Don't look at your cards before you have to, and don't follow obvious betting patterns
- Learn the lingo, how to shuffle and how to look at your cards
- Play nicely, and when you're mentally prepared
- Then read this book again

Getting better at poker is the easy part. It's winning that's hard

Glossary

A-Z of poker terminology

Action (1) The live player's turn to act (i.e. the action is on you). (2) A hand with lots of active players, and betting is said to have a lot of action.

All-in To make a bet that commits all your remaining chips to the pot.

Ante A mandatory bet enforced upon all players wishing to participate in the next hand.

Backdoor To complete your final hand using both the turn (fourth) and the river (fifth) community cards in a Hold'em game.

Bad beat To go into a confrontation with a huge advantage over your opponent, but still get beaten – against massive odds.

Bankroll The amount of money you have available for gambling.

Big blind The larger of the two blinds typically used in a Hold'em game in place of an ante.

Big slick A nickname for pocket A-K held in a Texas Hold'em game.

Blind A mandatory bet made by one or more players before any cards are dealt. Typically, blinds are made by players immediately to the left of the button.

Bluff To make a bet or raise when it's unlikely that you're holding the best hand.

Board Describes all the community cards appearing in a Hold'em game.

Boat A full house.

Bot Abbreviation of Robot. Refers to the software designed for playing poker.

Bubble The last finishing position in a tournament which doesn't win anything (e.g. to come twenty-first in a game when the top 20 only are paid).

Burn To protect the integrity of the deck by discarding the top card face-down before dealing to a community board.

Button A plastic disc – typically marked with a 'D' or 'Dealer' – that is passed around the table, indicating the order of play. The player with the dealer button is said to be on the button.

Buy-in The cost of participating in a tournament.

Call To equal the bet made before you and therefore continue as an active player in the hand.

Calling station A passive player who likes to call every bet but who rarely folds or raises.

Cap In a game with a limit on raises per betting round, the cap is the final raise in that sequence.

Cash out To leave a cash game and turn chips back into cash.

Check With no bets before a player, he can check to pass the action to the next player in sequence without taking any action. Betting chips may also be referred to as checks.

Check-raise To check in a deliberate attempt to induce a bet from following players, and then raise over that bet.

Connector A starting pair in a Hold'em game where the cards are consecutive (e.g. 6-7, J-Q).

Crack To beat a powerful hand.

Cut-off The player who is one position before the dealer or button.

Dead card A card no longer playable. Similarly a dead hand is a hand no longer playable.

Dead money A derogatory term used to describe players identified as having no real chance of winning.

Deuce A Two – the lowest-ranking card in poker.

Dominated To dominate is to hold the same best

card as your opponent, but with a stronger kicker (e.g. A-4 is dominated by A-Q).

Draw To draw is to need a specific card or cards to change your hand to a winning one (e.g. in Texas Hold'em, if you hold A-K with a flop of Q-J-4 you could be said to be drawing to a straight – requiring a Ten to make a strong hand).

Drawing dead To be against an opponent who cannot be beaten, regardless of more community cards to come.

Family pot A pot in which all the players on the table are still involved and live before the flop.

Fish A derogatory term used to describe a poorer player who gives his money away too easily. You will often hear the phrase 'don't tap on the aquarium' in reference to fish when players welcome them – and their money - at the table, and don't want them scared away.

Flop The first three community cards, delivered face-up simultaneously.

Flush Five cards of the same suit.

Flush draw To hold four cards of one suit, hoping to hit a fifth to make the flush.

Fold To withdraw from that hand by giving your cards back to the dealer.

Four-of-a-kind Four cards of the same rank.

Free card When all players check a round of betting before the turn or river card, that card is referred to as a free card.

Freeroll A tournament with no entry cost.

Freezeout A tournament structure where each player receives the same amount of chips, and plays until only one player remains.

Full house Any three-of-a-kind, plus a pair of a different rank.

Gutshot A card drawn to complete an inside straight.

Heads-up When a single pot is contested between only two players, or when a tournament is down to the last two players.

Hole card A player's concealed cards.

House The casino, card room or establishment running the game.

Implied odds Pot odds that don't yet exist, but which might be calculated and expected before the end of the hand. Implied odds calculations include the number of players you expect to remain live by the end of the hand, and their contributions to the pot.

Inside straight Four cards, requiring one in the middle to complete a straight (e.g. 4, 5, x, 7, 8)

Into the tank An expression used when a player is thinking for a long time about his hand; he goes into the tank.

Joker Often used as a wild card. The 53rd card in the deck.

Junk Poor cards. See also **Rags**.

Kicker In near-equivalent hands, the kicker is the player's highest unpaired card, and is used to determine the winner (e.g. Iif you hold Q-J and your opponent holds Q-9, and you both make a pair of Queens on the flop, your Jack kicker wins you the hand).

Limp A flat call to a bet. Generally used to describe pre-flop action. The player might be referred to as a limper.

Live Live cards that can still win a hand for you when you are the underdog. If you hold Q-7 and your opponent holds Q-J, your Queen is dead but the Seven could still make you a winning pair and is thus considered live.

Loose To play more hands than normal.

Lowball A poker variant where the lowest hand wins.

Made hand A completed hand (i.e. a made straight on the flop) that requires no further drawing cards.

Maniac A very aggressive and over-active player. A maniac gets involved in lots of pots with plenty of raising, betting and bluffing. Often seen early in tournament play as players attempt to amass an early chip lead.

Monster A powerful hand, almost certain to win.

Muck Discarded and burnt cards held by the dealer. Also describes the action of folding – 'he mucked his hand'.

No-limit Any variant of poker where there is no limit on the maximum raise allowed, up to and including all that player's chips.

Nuts The best possible hand in the current situation. Also applied to specific hand rankings (e.g. to have the nuts straight or nut flush).

Off-suit A Hold'em starting hand with two cards of different suits.

Omaha A flop game where each player receives four cards, and must combine two of these with three from a five-card board to make the best five-card poker hand.

Open-ended straight Four cards, consecutive in sequence, requiring one at either end to make a straight.

Option The player posting the big blind has the option to raise or check in sequence.

Out An out or outs describes the card or cards that you need in order to change your hand to a winning one. If you need a heart to win and there are nine left in the deck, you have nine outs.

Overcard A card on the community board that's higher than those you currently hold. If you hold 9-J and the flop comes 7-Q-K, there are two overcards on the board.

Pair Two cards of the same rank.

Pass To fold.

Play the board When the community cards represent the best hand you can make, you play the board. Most likely when the board produces a very strong hand such as a full house. It often results in a split pot between players, each playing the board.

Pocket The cards that are dealt to you, and you alone. Also called the hole.

Pocket pair A made pair dealt to you in a Hold'em game. If you are dealt 7-7 you have pocket Sevens as your pocket pair.

Post To put in a blind bet.

Pot-committed A situation where you have so many of your chips invested on the pot that you are locked into it.

Pot-limit A variant in which the maximum bet is limited by the amount already in the pot.

Pot odds The amount of money in the pot compared to the amount you must pay to continue playing. If it costs you $5 to remain in a pot worth $50, you are getting 10-1 pot odds for your call. If the odds of your hand winning reflect the pot odds, a call would be correct.

Quads Four-of-a-kind.

Ragged A relatively random flop (or board) that wouldn't appear to have helped anybody (e.g. Jd-6h-2c would look ragged).

Rags Worthless cards.

Rainbow A rainbow flop is one that contains three different suits. No flush can be made on the turn alone.

Raise To match and then increase the previous bet.

Rake The amount of money taken from every pot by the dealer.

Rank The numerical value of a card, as opposed to its suit.

Rebuy Many tournaments will offer the chance to buy back into a tournament – once or many times – when a player has lost all his chips. Rebuys are often also time-restricted (e.g. unlimited rebuys for the first hour of play).

Represent To play in a style that represents a card not actually held (e.g. to check until a King arrives on the turn, and then bet as if it's hit your own hand).

Reraise To raise a raise.

Ring game A cash game as opposed to a tournament game.

River The fifth and final community card, also known as fifth street.

Rock A very tight player who will never play anything but a premium hand.

Royal flush The best hand possible, 10-J-Q-K-A suited.

Runner-runner A hand made with the last two community cards.

Satellite A tournament that offers a seat in a much larger tournament as its prize instead of cash.

Scare card A community card that could make a previously strong hand no longer the favourite to win (e.g. if you held pocket Kings, but the turn card brings an Ace, you can no longer assume K-K is winning).

Second pair A pair made with the second highest card within the flop (e.g. if you hold J-9 and the flop comes Q-9-3, you have the second pair).

Semi-bluff A bet or raise that you hope will be folded to, but is done with a hand that at least has a number of chances to win if called.

Set A three-of-a-kind formed by a pocket pair and a matching rank on the board.

Seventh street The final round of betting in Seven-card Stud.

Short stack An amount of chips low in value compared to others at the table. A player might be referred to as the short stack at the table.

Showdown When all the players left in a hand turn their cards over to determine who has won. This is only done after the final betting round has been completed, with at least two active players still in the pot.

Side pot A side pot is created when one player is all-in for his entire chip stack, but other players still have money with which to bet. The all-in player is only eligible for an amount equivalent to the chips he invested, so any further betting goes into a side pot between the remaining live players.

Slow play An act of subterfuge. To play a very strong hand slowly to mislead other players, perhaps to stay in the pot longer than if they sensed a strong opposing hand.

Small blind The smaller of the two mandatory bets typically used in a Hold'em game.

Soft-play Going easy on a player for reasons outside the game (e.g. to allow a friend to get away from a losing hand cheaply). Unacceptable in any game.

Splash the pot An unpopular move when chips are thrown directly into the main pot instead of being placed in front of them.

Split pot Two or more players with equivalent hands which split the pot equally.

Steal To bluff in a late position in an attempt to steal the pot from apparently weak hands.

Straddle A rare live game bet – typically made by the player sitting to the immediate left of the big blind – equal to twice the big blind. This acts as a raise, with the action starting to the left of the raising player once the hole cards have been dealt.

Straight Five sequentially consecutive cards of mixed suit.

Straight flush Five sequentially consecutive cards of the same suit.

String bet When making a bet or a raise, all the chips must be moved in front of the player. To put some chips forward and then go back to your stack for more is called a string bet, and is not allowed. This is to prevent the player putting out feelers and watching for opponents' reactions as the amount of the bet gets bigger.

Stud Any variant of poker where the first card or cards are dealt face-down, with subsequent cards being dealt face-up.

Suited To have a starting hand in a Hold'em game where two cards are of the same suit.

Tell A behavioural clue from a player about the strength of their hand, or their intended action. Often caused by nerves.

Tight A conservative player who only plays strong hands. Unlikely to bluff when he bets.

Tilt Commonly seen after a bad loss, a player on tilt will play recklessly and wildly. A tilting player might get involved in too many hands, bluff outrageously, or raise with weak hands.

Top pair To form a pair using the highest card in the flop (e.g. you hold J-9 and the flop comes J-5-2).

Top set To form the highest possible three of a kind (e.g. you hold J-J and the flop comes J-8-6).

Trey A three.

Trips Three-of-a-kind.

Turn The fourth community card, also known as fourth street.

Underdog The player with the hand least likely to win mathematically.

Under the gun To be the player who must act first in any betting round. Considered the weakest position because you must make a decision with no information available to you about your opponents' actions.

WPT Abbreviation for the World Poker Tour, one of the biggest organizations in the poker world.

Wheel A straight sequence, e.g. A-2-3-4-5.

Learn your poker jargon and you'll be at home in the Vegas casinos

Further Reading

If you want to take your game further you should try...

Harrington on Hold'em Volumes 1 and 2
Dan Harrington and Bill Robertie
Feted by the experts as the book to buy if you're serious about tournament Hold'em. The first volume takes you up to the final table and the second tells you what to do when you get there.

Super System 2
Doyle Brunson
Doyle Brunson's original Super System changed the face of poker for ever and although the sequel doesn't add much it's a lesson in aggression. Sections on all the major poker variants.

The Theory of Poker
David Sklansky
Not for the beginner, Sklansky's book is a must for any budding pro.

Hold'em for Advanced Players
David Sklansky and Mason Malmuth
Another must-buy for serious players from the renowned master strategist. Chris 'Jesus' Ferguson, one of the world's most successful poker, pros recommends this as his number-one choice of book.

Caro's Book of Poker Tells
Mike Caro
A book that relies on photographs and accompanying descriptions to show you what to look out for in other players. There's no other book on tells that comes even close to this one.

Online Ace
Scott Fischman
Traditional strategy books haven't delved much into the online world but Fischman's book is a masterclass from one of the world's most successful players.

Shut Up and Deal
Jesse May
There aren't many narrative books around that are worth reading but this is one of them. A classic, although it might put you off turning pro for ever.

The Man Behind the Shades
Nolan Dalla and Peter Alson
Stu Ungar was probably the world's most natural card player but his life swung from moments of genius to moments of tragedy. This is his story and it's one of the best reads in the poker world.

Swimming with the Devilfish
Des Wilson
A brilliant look at the underground British poker scene with an extended biography of the UK's most successful player, Dave 'Devilfish' Ulliott. Proof that poker's not just an American game.

Aces and Kings
Michael Kaplan and Brad Reagan
A look at the lives of the world's most successful poker players, from one of the best poker writers in the industry.

Index

About the Authors

Dave Woods is the Editor-in-Chief of the UK's leading poker magazine, *PokerPlayer*. He's also a frighteningly keen and competitive player. Turned on to cards at an early age by his parents, he's progressed from playing cribbage and Newmarket for pennies to contesting million-dollar pots at major international tournaments like the Aussie Millions. If he's not in Vegas or the card rooms of London, he can be found trawling the online poker sites for potential victims. He's now decided to teach you everything he knows.

Matt Broughton was one of the early adopters of Internet poker and has been boring the hell out of everybody about it ever since. A freelance journalist and one of the expert presenters on the award-winning *Poker Night Live* TV show, Matt has contributed to just about every poker magazine there is. A frequent visitor to Las Vegas, Matt can also be found participating in many of the UK's private games networks. He is the host of www.pokerbods.com and also runs his own poker events and poker table companies.

Picture Credits

The publishers would like to thank the following sources for their kind permission to reproduce the pictures in this book.

Alamy Images: /Barry Bland: 140; /Cut and Deal Ltd: 84, 158, 163, 181: /Darren Matthews: 57; /Niall McDiarmid: 123; /Purcell Team: 186; /Teena Taylor: 152; /Jochem Wijnands/ Picture Contact: 180 bl

Carlton Books Ltd: 127, 179 br

Corbis Images: /Miguel Gandert: 73; /Kim Kulish: 142

Getty Images: 91; /Todd Bigelow: 96, 103; /Buyenlarge/Time Life Pictures: 14; /Frank Driggs Collection: 178; /Matt Henry Gunther/Stone: 60; /Ethan Miller: 22, 23, 27, 72, 85, 134, 136, 166, 170; /Robert Mora: 9; /Larry W Smith: 21. 102; /Peter Stackpole/Time Life Pictures: 42

MANSIONpoker.com: /Speed Poker: 169 t

New Line Home Entertainment: 24

Picture Desk/The Kobal Collection: 12; /IRS Media/AM Playhouse: 6; /Miramax: 167; /Universal: 58, 164; /Warner Brothers: 132, 172

Pokerimages.com: 95; /Ulvis Alberts: 56; /Bill Burlington: 8 bl, 11, 19, 20, 76, 176 br, 180 tl , 180 tr; /Paul Ress: 171, 179 bl

Private Collection: 8 tr, 143, 144, 149

Rex Features: /Andrew Drysdale: 113, 175 br; /Everett Collection: 40, 70, 86, 106, 124, 150; /Matt Phelvin: 126, 128; /Snap: 4

Richard Bosworth Photography: 10

Stock.XCHNG: 120, 169 br, 174 l, 174 r, 175 br, 176tr, 177, 180 br

Every effort has been made to acknowledge correctly and contact the source and/or copyright holder of each picture and Carlton Books Limited apologises for any unintentional errors of omissions which will be corrected in future editions of the book.